WHAT PEOPLE ARE S

TOO GOOD TO BE TRUE

How do you preach the death of God? In this powerful collection of sermons Chris Rodkey plunges deep into the tradition of radical Christianity from Tillich to Altizer to Rollins to fashion something entirely refreshing and new. These are personal, contemporary, and at the same time profoundly biblical sermons. Anyone who preaches the Gospel and still has a spark of intellectual curiosity will want to read this book.

Clayton Crockett, Associate Professor and Director of Religious Studies, University of Central Arkansas

Chris Rodkey presents a radical vision of the preacher's task. Preachers are called to unmask the popular gods of culture and the church to reveal the lively, changing, and unbounded living God uncontained by dogma, institution, or profession. Chris Rodkey's lectionary commentaries provide an alternative theological vision which will inspire preachers toward prophetic innovation and homiletic excellence. Postmodernism demands more – and better – theology and not less theological reflection. Chris provides solid theological soul food for preachers and congregations. The old gods have died but a lively iconoclastic "Christian atheism" gives birth to healthy, life-transforming, and Earth-affirming visions of God when they are most desperately needed. Chris gives us one such vision.

Chris Rodkey has charted a path that you may follow at your own peril, but only a risk-taking theology can provide us with the spiritual nurture and challenge we need today.

Bruce Epperly, author of *Process Theology: A Guide for the Perplexed* and *Healing Marks: Spirituality and Healing in Mark's Gospel*

I find it rather peculiar that practitioners and pastors frequently ask whether or not radical theology can or should play a role in today's churches, as if the subversive kernel of Christianity has at some point been something other than radical. To even ask such a question is to acknowledge that the actually existing churches, out of their perpetual love affair with power and privilege, have domesticated the radical truth of Christianity at nearly every turn.

However, in this provocative and important book, Chris Rodkey boldly picks up the mantle of Thomas Altizer and Paul Tillich in order to remind us that the subversive truth of Christianity has always been radical, which in turn leads practitioners and pastors to ask a better question – namely, if those of us in the churches don't think it necessary to express the subversive, radical truth of Christianity in our sermons and our liturgies then, really, why are we preaching, and why should we continue to worship a domesticated God? Readers will come away with a fresh understanding of radical theology and preachers will find practical tools to develop a more radical, and thus more Christian, homiletic.

This book deserves a wide audience and should be read by everyone who cares about the transformative art of preaching.
Phil Snider is Sr. Minister of Brentwood Christian Church in Springfield, MO, and the author of, most recently, *Preaching After God: Derrida, Caputo and the Language of Postmodern Homiletics.*

Too Good to be True

Radical Christian Preaching,
Year A

Too Good to be True

Radical Christian Preaching, Year A

Christopher D. Rodkey

CHRISTIAN
ALTERNATIVE

Winchester, UK
Washington, USA

First published by Christian Alternative Books, 2014
Christian Alternative Books is an imprint of John Hunt Publishing Ltd.,
Laurel House, Station Approach,
Alresford, Hants, SO24 9JH, UK
office1@jhpbooks.net
www.johnhuntpublishing.com
www.christian-alternative.com

For distributor details and how to order please visit the 'Ordering' section on our website.

ISBN: 978 1 78279 130 0

A CIP catalogue record for this book is available from the British Library.

Design: Stuart Davies

Printed and bound by CPI Group (UK) Ltd, Croydon, CR0 4YY

We operate a distinctive and ethical publishing philosophy in all areas of our business, from our global network of authors to production and worldwide distribution.

CONTENTS

Foreword

Peter Rollins

One of the marks of truly great thinkers in any given tradition is that they are read seriously across various traditions. The message of individuals such as Darwin, Newton, and Nietzsche was not constrained by their respective disciplines but caused deep and lasting reverberations across numerous disciplines. Science, art, politics and philosophy were no longer the same in their aftermath.

The work of such people is like a flood that overflows the riverbeds of their particular training and sweeps away outdated, fossilized orthodoxies. A flood that clears the way for new, innovative and liberating practices to emerge.

In an analogous way a great movement reaches beyond the particular interests of a single group and speaks to people not immediately associated with it. From the French Revolution to the Arab Spring, revolutionary movements cut across old party lines and speak of a liberation that joins together previously disconnected individuals.

It is this mark that was almost completely missing from thinkers and movements located within theology and church life during the twentieth century. Unlike the century before it theology and church practice in the twentieth century was mostly only of interest to those located safely within the walls of seminaries and denominations.

However, there are some exceptions to this rule. In theological theory one of these exceptions was witnessed in a brief period of time between the late 1950s through to the 1960s. This was a time when a theological movement made an explosive impact on the wider cultural scene. Some of the most notable names in this movement were Paul Tillich and Thomas Altizer in the United States—both of whom received front-page coverage on *Time* magazine—and John Robinson and Don Cupitt in the United Kingdom.

These were not superficial apologists of religion but rather serious thinkers and practitioners, whose "death of God" theology caused such a scandal that they sparked off passionate discussions on the nature of faith and life in supposedly avowedly secular spaces. While the Christian proclamation of God's death was a complex one, it spoke to people in an immediate and personal way. The cryptic utterances of the radical theologians reached far beyond the narrow confines of the church and were taken seriously, for a time, by society at large.

Yet this surprising theological event was short-lived, and the flood that threatened to wash away old orthodoxies was first contained and then pushed back. In the aftermath of this singular moment there was a great reversal in which the Religious Right came into being and, in the name of a universal message, restricted what went under the name of "theology" to a form of inane tribal apologetics.

In terms of a Christian practice in the twentieth century that broke free from narrow denominational confines to speak beyond traditional borders an obvious example is Alcoholics Anonymous. This movement, founded by Bill Wilson and Bob Smith, spoke to people from all walks of life, whether theists or atheists, liberals or conservatives, rich or poor.

AA, along with other twelve-step programs, are populated by those who feel like the trash of the world (one of Paul's most potent definitions of the Christian) and thus are able to welcome all who seek help in overcoming addiction. In contrast to communities that find strength through externalizing problems, blaming brokenness on some scapegoat, twelve-step programs are built upon an invitation to own up to one's own brokenness and to face it squarely.

While deeply successful in helping to transform lives, the white-hot insight that underpinned their principles did not make a serious impact in the actually existing church. They may continue to meet in the basements of religious buildings, but the message still does not seem to have reached up to the sanctuary.

Thankfully both radical theology and various twelve-step programs are still alive and well. The problem, however, is that their universality has been somewhat tamed. The radical theology movement retreated behind the walls of the academy while twelve-step programs quietly focused on their respective aims.

I am too young to have witnessed the birth of AA in the 1930s or the ascension of radical theology in the '60s. But when I finally did come across them I found two sites that seemed pregnant with soteriological possibilities. In radical theology I found a type of thinking whose time was yet to come, and in AA I saw underlying principles that could be of use to all people struggling with life. While I came to both after I was already pursuing my own project, both have helped me to reinterpret, develop, and situate my own work.

It is my hope that the apocalyptic power held in the theory of Radical Theology and the underlying principles of AA can combine in the twenty-first century to re-ignite the fire that almost set the world ablaze in the 1960s.

This is where I situate a book like the one you hold in your hands. Here we witness a beautifully-crafted work with the power to speak beyond the walls of the actually existing church. A message aimed squarely at our hearts while not patronizing our minds. A message that calls us to strip away our false certainties, embrace our brokenness, face death, and celebrate life.

Christopher Rodkey is part of a small, but growing, group of visionaries who are proclaiming a passionate, life-giving theological word, a word that could make fertile again the desert that is church today.

This is a living word, one that has the potential to overflow the boundaries that separate "believers" from "unbelievers," liberals from conservatives, and churchgoers from those who would never darken the door of a sanctuary.

This message exists today in various forms. But for it to truly make an impact we need it to touch the lives of people beyond the walls of the academy: *we need it to preach.*

This book is firmly rooted in the tradition of Tillich, not only in the way that it draws inspiration from some of his ideas, but also in the way that it too takes seriously the need to let these ideas breathe in the pulpit. Rodkey's book presents the message of radical theology in a way that can challenge us to confront our darkness, think seriously, and act responsibly so that we might discover a new depth of life.

You stand at the threshold of this book and so I encourage you to read it with an open heart and active mind. If you do this, by the end, you will find yourself at another threshold. For you will be standing before the potential held within the pages of this book; a new event that is not-yet. It is at this point that we must challenge ourselves concerning whether we might commit ourselves to this event, becoming part of the next generation of preachers willing to proclaim this scandalous word to the world.

Pentecosting:
Preaching the Death of God

The language of preaching must be theologically apt. *Preaching is
doing theology.*
David Buttrick[1]

*A minister functions within the visible church by attending to that
which is invisible.*

*That which is in-visible adds to the meaning of our experience and
alters the quality of life.*

*We cannot know the in-visible church without inward thinking and
downward thinking.*
Charles Winquist[2]

*To speak of the death of God means ... that finally at the end of the
Christian phase of Western culture, the reality of the living God is
freed from the cultural concepts and other institutions that attempt
to objectify and domesticate it. The death of God marks the end of
Christian culture and, especially, of its attempt to assimilate ... the
living God of whom our religion as well as our diffuse religiosity is
a desperate caricature. This means that, man being a religious
animal, we are groping for a new concept of God and a new attitude,
a mode of being congruous with it; that a new religiosity is
dawning. And a new era begins when a new religiosity appears,
rises from the empty tomb of the dead God.*
Gabriel Vahanian[3]

One of the pervasive criticisms of radical Christian theology is
that it is out of touch with the common person and is impractical
to the life of a clergyperson. Even Thomas Altizer's ideas were

forbidden from being taught in Methodist theological schools by Methodist bishops in the late 1960s.[4] The fact is that radical Christian theology is *not* unthinkable or unapproachable by those within the churches, but it is repressed and ignored because those with power have the most to lose in the church.

Instead of taking the radical aspects of its own theology seriously beginning with Paul Tillich, the church has since his death generally elected to go into its own un-theological directions, claiming that because of the threat of radical theology, the church must retreat into a new kind of evangelicalism to survive. This new evangelicalism has branded anything different than whatever resided within the safety of its own porous boundaries as heresy: anything theologically "different" was branded as *radical*.

Evangelicalism required a caricature of radicalism to expand and thrive. In doing so, evangelicalism manifested its own destiny: decline, stagnancy, *rigor mortis*. A stiffening of the boundaries, a *necrophilia*, or lust for death.[5] This is easily demonstrated by considering what cultural influences define evangelicalism today. Evangelicalism is influenced by politicians, demagogues, radio talk show hosts, and the repressive social apparatus known as the Christian bookstore industry: *Principalities, powers, and spiritual wickedness in high places.*[6] Preachers may think they are defining the conservatism of our time, but they are really surfing a wave from someone else's wave machine.

In response, "liberal" or so-called "progressive" preachers are attempting to use modern and historically-informed approaches to their craft, indulging in the so-called "historical Jesus," and stripes of theology that could potentially be radical, but usually just become a different way to say the same things, such as the many varieties of liberation theology. In our post-colonial academic era, cultural relativism is the new Patriarch. We have returned to preaching our feelings. As Jonathan Edwards warned, if we move into these directions, our affections are all that remain.

But what do I mean by "radical" theology? By this I mean theology that follows the lure, or the call, of an apocalyptic Christian worldview that God is radically changing, and along with God, we must change as well. And this change is not just a self-transcendence or intersubjective paradigm shift, but a *radical change* which carries and demands tremendous social and political consequences. *Radical theology is blasphemous* to the orthodoxy because radicalism points out the hypocrisy at the center of religious power. *Radical theology practices blasphemy*, as it reclaims Jesus as not only a radical preacher, but Jesus representing and incarnating a God radically moving forward in history.

It is on this point that radical theology preaches the death of God. We should remember that in Friedrich Nietzsche's *The Gay Science*, the philosopher told the following infamous parable:

Have you not heard of that madman who lit a lantern in the bright morning hours, ran to the market place, and cried incessantly: "I seek God! I seek God!" —As many of those who did not believe in God were standing around just then, he provoked much laughter. Has he got lost? asked one. Did he lose his way like a child? asked another. Or is he hiding? Is he afraid of us? Has he gone on a voyage? Emigrated? —Thus they yelled and laughed.

The madman jumped into their midst and pierced them with his eyes. "Whither is God?" he cried; "I will tell you. *We have killed him*—you and I. All of us are his murderers. But how did we do this? How could we drink up the sea? Who gave us the sponge to wipe away the entire horizon? What were we doing when we unchained this earth from its sun? Whither is it moving now? Whither are we moving? Away from all suns?

Are we not plunging continually? Backward, sideward, forward, in all directions? Is there still any up or down? Are we not straying as through an infinite nothing? Do we not feel the breath of empty space? Has it not become colder? Is not night continually closing in on us? Do we not need to light lanterns in the morning? Do we hear nothing as yet of the gravediggers who are burying God? Do we smell nothing as yet of the divine decomposition? Gods, too, decompose. God is dead. God remains dead. And we have killed him.

"How shall we comfort ourselves, the murderers of all murderers? What was holiest and mightiest of all that the world has yet owned has bled to death under our knives: who will wipe this blood off us? What water is there for us to clean ourselves? What festivals of atonement, what sacred games shall we have to invent?" ...

Here the madman fell silent and looked again at his listeners; and they, too, were silent and stared at him in astonishment. At last he threw his lantern on the ground, and it broke into pieces and went out. "I have come too early," he said then; "my time is not yet. This tremendous event is still on its way, still wandering; it has not yet reached the ears of men. Lightning and thunder require time; the light of the stars requires time; deeds, though done, still require time to be seen and heard. This deed is still more distant from them than the most distant stars — *and yet they have done it themselves.*"

It has been related further that on the same day the madman forced his way into several churches and there struck up his *requiem aeternam deo.* Led out and called to account, he is said always to have replied nothing but: "What after all are these churches now if they are not the tombs and sepulchers of God?"[7]

There is much to say about these words which have so deeply influenced the history of ideas, but for now I raise the following points. Nietzsche *did not* say that there is no God: he *did not* say that he does not believe in a God. Nor did Nietzsche say that there is a God. In Nietzsche's parable, the only one who walks into any of the churches is the madman, and the conservative townsfolk who flippantly dismiss his questions remain in the realm of commerce. They mock him, and continue their shopping.

Nietzsche's madman knows the words to the mass. The madman asks: "What are these churches now if not the tombs and sepulchers of God?" Are the noises of hymns little more than the gravediggers burying God?

Our so-called "contemporary" church movement affirms Nietzsche's parable. Indeed, the evangelical mega-churches are quite Victorian in their commemoration of the death of God. As Mark C. Taylor writes, tombs are erected to remember so we don't have to remember.[8] The anti-sacramentalism of our contemporary church movement also reflects the smell of divine decomposition: we don't have to re-member a death of God, because there is nothing left to dis-member. This God is long gone. It would seem that the shadow of God worshiped by the nihilistic American fundamentalism of Christianity, transcendent and totalitarian as ever, is no longer a God who shatters out of Godself a genuine and full incarnation. This image of God reflects the political hopes of conservative Christianity, a mighty fortress, staunch and unchanging, beyond reproach and largely inaccessible, but a personal God who is there as a cosmic Santa Claus when conveniently needed to thank or cling to in times of crisis.

So where does this leave the one called to preach a genuine Gospel, and reclaim the blasphemous core of Christian preaching?

First, before going any further, I wish to pronounce openly

that preaching is a contextual act, and a liturgical act. Preaching happens within the context of worship. That worship can occur anywhere, but preaching is a sacramental act among other sacramental acts, and preaching must come from the context of the preacher's own worship. The spirituality of the preacher itself demands a life of worship, and a lifestyle of liturgical living.[9] But for the radical preacher, this context of worship must also be as self-reflective as it is theological, and if having no other community is done in solitude amongst a community of other readers, practitioners, and theologians. Our local contexts may be very different, and our local issues may be foreign to one another, but our commitment to the Gospel as a radical movement is part of our commitment to the church universal.

Second, radical Christian preaching must declare the Good News of the death of God as the basis of an incarnational faith. A full and apocalyptic understanding of the doctrine of the trinity is impossible apart from a Christian faith in a kenotic incarnation. Christ is the center of Gospel preaching, and it is this same Christ who is God-made-flesh. This Christ is not a "mode" or "modal person" of God, but is himself God. It is the radical position that orthodox Christianity denies the fullness of Christ's divinity by rejecting an actual change of God at the moment of Christmas, the incarnation of Christ. The radical critique of "liberal" Christology is that liberals usually either deny the divinity of Jesus (that is, *psilanthropism* or "adoptionism") or overemphasize the patriarchy of God by removing all possible attributes or natures from God, especially gendered attributes (that is, *monarchianism*).

While I respect much of what contemporary theologians have attempted to accomplish with regard to the gender of God, and at some points these theologians' ideas are radical, the ironic result is often a denial of certain kinds of genderings or racial understandings of God in favor of other genderings, queerings, or racial understandings. The theologian might admit that "all" are legitimate, but the theologian is not being honest; Mary Daly called this dishonesty a "re-labeling."[10] By simply re-labeling, the theologian's image is always prioritized, and in doing so the station of the transcendent God is always elevated to an alien transcendence that can only be approached by metaphorical language. The power of symbols, the theory of which Tillich so painstakingly developed over his lifetime, is completely robbed by the inaccessibility of God and the banality of language to describe the divine.

The scholar might ask, how is the alternative not the heresy of *patripassianism*, or the idea that God the Father suffers on the cross? God the Father does not suffer on the cross, because God the Father has already incarnated in the incarnation. The birth of God the Son is absolutely necessary as the apocalyptic move from God the Father pouring out into God the Son. God the Son suffers on the cross. The fullness of God*head* dies on the cross.

To this end, third, radical preaching must have the crucifixion at the center of its images: *preaching Christ crucified.*[11] Obviously, not every sermon must exegete the crucifixion, but the crucifixion must be the lens through which radical interpretations of scripture must be read. We live in a world of crucifixion, a world of continuing crucifixion. The Good News is that the Christ-event of God's death on the cross may lead us to take up our own crosses and imitate Christ through self-sacrifice and doing the hard work of building the Kingdom of God, but the Bad News is that the church and its inhabitants have failed throughout history to do just this. As a result, our world is a world of Bad News; Bad News largely enabled by those preaching the "Good News." When a child dies of hunger or at the hands of violence, God dies. The crucifixion continues at the hand of the authorities. The call of radical preaching is to accomplish the meaning of the crucifixion, forsaking transcendence ("My God, My God, why have you forsaken me?")[12] and being willing to step into a descent into Hell by way of the cross, to search for a genuine resurrection of flesh in Easter.

Fourth, radical preaching understands that the enemy of Christianity is usually inside of the church. Carefully recognizing the anti-Semitism and anti-Judaism of the New Testament when it comes to the Jews and the "Temple," the core of Jesus' critique regarding the religious of his time is not a criticism that may only be applied to the Jews of his time. To the contrary, and to state the obvious, religious hypocrisy is everywhere, always beginning with ourselves. Our unwillingness to name and claim it for ourselves kills God by continuing the crucifixion.

It is on this point where American forms of atheism, the so-called "new" atheism, need to be addressed from pulpits. As radical Christianity became marginalized in the 1960s at the beginning of the new evangelicalism and mega-church movements, a new scapegoat was required to fuel constituents' fears: secularism, and later atheism. This, of course, led to new forms of evangelical atheisms.[13] In the past few months, for example, in my home state of Pennsylvania, one of the leaders of the state's primary atheist advocacy organization announced plans to desecrate the Qur'an as a protest against the state legis-lature's declaration of a "Year of Religious Diversity."[14] Deep down, this atheist and his organization are embodying what many evangelicals wish they could do, and their inability to do this in public is the fault of the so-called "liberal media" who would shame them for doing so. Many evangelicals, too, scoff at the reality of religious diversity, and wish they could simply legislate or prioritize their own.

Again, what this particular atheist group is attempting is not very different than what many evangelicals wish they had license to do.[15] This new atheism is a product or by-product of the church. Even when atheism expresses itself as an innocent humanism, it castrates liberal Christianities as little more than a humanism "with God added." Its own product is required by evangelicalism. Evangelicals believe that they will receive the

Mark of Cain in this rivalry because of their faithfulness, but we should recall that the one whose offerings were more pleasing to God ultimately perished.[16]

But, fifth, radical theology *requires the practice of a Christian atheism*. To follow with our earlier discussion of atheism, a Christian atheism acknowledges that if we are truly worshiping the divine, we cannot simply say that all is divine and worship the encompassing whole of all that claims divinity. We pick and choose. I do not worship the god of Christian evangelicalism; in fact, I emphatically reject this god. Or at least I *attempt* to reject it. Similarly, I choose not to worship the God of capitalism. I am an atheist in this regard. But my atheism never quite measures up to the atheism demanded by the God whose death points us toward the final and ultimate joy of the cross. I, along with others, *fail* at my call to be a Christian atheist, as a true Christian faith requires atheism. Preaching is one way we openly proclaim our rejection of certain gods, as well as our *inability* to reject other deities.

To practice atheism faithfully requires radical doubt in our preaching. As a child and teenager I heard countless sermons about how having true and real faith leads to a life of abundance and happiness; this theology is often called the Gospel of Wealth. The insanity of this preaching—popularized everywhere Christianity is "comfortable"[17]—is emphasized by anyone asking the question of evil or theodicy: why, then, do bad things happen to good people? The preacher usually answers this, sometimes at funerals for young people, proclaiming evil to be part of God's big plan that is not open to question, or by pointing to the book of Job, knowing that his adherent is not going to really read the text.

Instead, the radical preacher teaches that doubt is necessary for belief. Again, as Tillich famously taught, if we have no doubt, we have a religion devoid of faith, reduced to arguments about history and not about life-changing ideas and world-changing paradigm shifts.[18] The earthquake of the resurrection is practiced in faith by looking for evidence of seismic events rather than asking what it means for the curtain of the temple to be torn and then searching out a means to live and embody a resurrection life.[19] In this way, as Peter Rollins so eloquently preaches, to simply accept the resurrection is to actually deny the resurrection, a denial of its power to change the world in substantial ways.[20]

Radicalism always has the possibility of going too far, and therefore must attempt to be accountable to others when possible, be derived out of a life of prayer and servitude, and be willing to change when errors are acknowledged. We should be careful not to proclaim a new Gospel, but proclaim and re-claim the Gospel newly.[21] Davidson Loehr, one of the great American radical preachers, writes that in preaching "we must engage the spirit of our times and the gods being served by our society, or else religion is too cowardly to respect."[22] Both Paul Tillich and Mary Daly have written extensively on existential and radical courage. Our *courage to be* may be regarded by others as *courage to sin*, but when preaching radically and with an unpopular message, we are in need of accountability and dialogue with others, so we may boldly, as Daly suggests, "re-call the courage to Sin Big."[23] Doing so cracks the fissures of structures which need to be torn down and reconstructed. This kind of blasphemy is the very core of the Gospel.

*

Prior to his declaration of the death of God, Nietzsche prefaced his parable with this short aphorism simply titled "In the horizon of the infinite":

We have left the land and have embarked. We have burned our bridges behind us—indeed, we have gone farther and destroyed the land behind us. Now, little ship, look out! Beside you is the ocean: to be sure, it does not always roar, and at times it lies spread out like silk and gold and reveries of graciousness. But hours will come when you will realize that it is infinite and that there is nothing more awesome than infinity. Oh, the poor bird that strikes the walls of this cage! Woe, when you feel homesick for the land as if it had offered more freedom—and there is no longer any "land."[24]

Radical theology is the call of the preacher to acknowledge that the Christian faith is an invitation to eat, breathe, and think God: sacramentally; breathing and practicing forgiveness and reconciliation;[25] and enacting God through words proclaimed in the dialectical uncertainty of the Eternal Now. We practice an offensive faith to the temple and to the empire. Offending is forward- and downward-moving; an enfleshed faith willing to take up the cross and descend into Hell with the hope and prayer for an Easter resurrection.

We may be homesick for the safety of Christendom, but the church no longer has a choice. We choose to imitate Christ, forward and downward. If we stay behind, we walk the plank. We journey together, for one of our implied cages is going it alone and enforcing the solitude of a genuine radicalism. A goal of preaching is to teach the audience how the church itself apprehends our apocalyptic hope and denies Christianity from truly being practiced.[26]

In December, 1967, in the midst of the "death of God" controversy in the media, Rev. Dow Kirkpatrick preached an Advent sermon on Job 23:1-9 and 2 Corinthians 1:19-20 at First Methodist Episcopal Church in Evanston, IL:

Whatever these men [the death of God theologians] mean by what they are saying, *they have caught us in the church without a living God that we can lay our hands on.*

Everything I have read—and I mean everything—critical of these men for saying God is dead, has failed to offer a rebuttal that has any semblance of life about Him.

A lot of noise is coming from preachers and laymen who are in churches that won't let a Negro in the front door. And don't feel smug, for the God so often worshiped here resembles us and our dead values more than He resembles anything living and worthy of the name of God.

Whatever the radical theologians mean, I say, the God which is worshiped so broadly these days, especially during Christmas, needs killing. The greatest affirmation faith can make is to declare in our time that He is dead ...

If we ever dare to tell one another what really is wrapped up in that baby born in Bethlehem; it will be the death of an impassive, impersonal, far-off-filler-of-our-wishes and explainer of what we can't explain. The God we so vigorously defend is so often a faceless cipher, sitting way out on the edges of our lives, neatly out of place—where we think we can find him, the few times we need him.[27]

Dow Kirkpatrick was one of the architects of the denominational merger that became the United Methodist Church and was an early voice for civil rights and the women's movement. His own congregation, whose name changed to "United Methodist," reflecting this denominational work, voted a few years after he preached this sermon to dismiss him. Ousted from one of the most prestigious pulpits in the country, he left the country to become a "missionary in reverse" to Latin America.[28]

Preaching insecurity is insecure. Radical theology and radical preaching requires a "theology of offense" as Paul Tillich once proclaimed, but an offense not simply knocking down the weakened church, for doing so is far too easy, but similarly pose an offense to the spiritual wickednesses of society itself, and yet go far deeper to the rotting stilts holding their pedestals.[29] Radical preaching re-claims, by pro-claiming and re-membering the dis-memberment of God in history, and as such seeks to turn this world upside down through the way of the cross. In our theology and in our preaching, we are to voyage to the depths of the Gospel to expose the nihilistic core of our present times. When Jesus attended a wedding in Cana and discovered temple purification jars, he did not destroy them, rather, he filled them with new wine, and prioritized the New.[30] The Kingdom of God requires an ecclesia or assembly. Our role is not to close the churches but to invite Nietzsche's madman, and transform it from the inside out. As Gabriel Vahanian writes, "True icono-clasm begins with oneself, with the smashing of one's own idols, *i.e.*, of one's superannuated conception of God, of faith and religious allegiance."[31] Radical theological preaching begins in the church and intends to culminate in the church. If this means closing buildings to respond faithfully, *so be it*: the Kingdom is far more important and our apocalyptic hope demands us to transfigure and completely rethink our communities of faith. This, I believe, will only happen through preaching. It is my hope that this text is not only helpful for your ministry and call to radical theology, but leads us into a support network and invariably into the building of the Kingdom.

*

The radical Christian preacher boldly proclaims the apocalyptic hope of the immanent Kingdom. The Kingdom is the New Creation Now Occurring, and is enfleshed as, and within, the church, but the church as a whole through the process and processes of Christendom has apprehended the true hope of the Kingdom. There are no shortages of examples of this through

17

history, though they may be a surprise or shocking for many Christians to understand that the alignment with power, which coincided with exclusivistic Trinitarian orthodoxy, cemented the church's inability to bring about substantial change leading to an actual Kingdom.

In our post-Christendom situation, the church is now at a decisive turning point: to grasp onto these orthodoxies of the past, only to be, as the Charlton Heston cliché goes, pried from our cold, dead hands; or to recognize that now, *this now*, is the Now that is New. Thomas Altizer writes:

> [E]ven as the Christian must look upon the collapse of the ancient world as the inevitable historical consequence of the birth of Christianity, so, too, the Christian must now look upon the collapse of the past as the way to an apocalyptic and eschatological future. Christianity, even as all religious ways, knows death as the way to life, and knows an actual passage through death as the way to an actual realization of life. (*Total Presence*, 92)

The secularization which evangelicalism and fundamentalism is fighting—this secularization which evangelicalism *invented*—is not only an emerging mission field but is a necessary moment in the scheme of history. The death of Christendom means that its old models of God, especially those models obsessed with a lust for death, must too die, and transfigure into something new.

The preaching moment in the weakened church, in the church proclaiming the death of God, speaks into the noise of nihilism perpetuated by value-systems of the state and temple, is a public call to think God Newly to believers in exile from the mainstream of religion and society. It should be no surprise that an apocalyptic faith based upon parables, as parabolic speech indicates a *reversal*, seeks to reverse the social order. Preaching the death of God re-calls the beatifications of the Beatitudes, charging the church to enact and embody this reversal.[32] In our weakened, marginalized position in society, we are now primed to transgress the status quo.

Like all subversive art, preaching is always situational, contextual, and *theonomous*, which is to say, stepping into the unknown and into uncertainty in dangerous ways. If our preaching is not genuinely transgressive within our communities and contexts, it is irrelevant or apprehends the apocalyptic hope at the center of the Christian faith. Is the church called to proclaim, while patting the middle- and upper-classes of Americans on their backs, to "abandon all apocalyptic hope" to "all who enter here" because of the church's allergy to thinking God anew?[33] Or will our preaching incite the theological imagination of our audiences to turn this world upside-down?

The death of God theology that emerged in the late 1960s has often been called a "language event," which is to say that what radical theology primarily addressed is the problem or limitation of religious language for the holy. The inadequacy of religious language is a clearly Biblical idea, and remains a primary task for systematic theology. Radical theologian Paul M. Van Buren, for example, developed an important model for interpreting religious language in his underappreciated book, *The Edge of Language*, and Gabriel Vahanian's most iconoclastic teaching is that the word "God" is the final idol which Christianity must overcome.[34]

David Buttrick, arguably the most important theologian of homiletics of our past century, says quite plainly in his classic *Homiletic: Moves and Structures* that because God is experienced as an absence, the void into which the preacher preaches is to speak in analogical terminology for the divine. The problem with this, of course, is that the God-talk poured into this void is idolatrous and venerates the opposite of God; "A turn of the radio dial on Sunday mornings," Buttrick mentions, "will let you hear all kinds of demonic God-talk!"[35] Since *Homiletic* was published in

1987, the perpetual, constant noise of God-talk has become increasingly demonic and Satanic. It has confused Spirit-filled boldness with certainty, cowardice, and mimetic victimization mechanisms.

Yet I propose that the death of God is a language-event which is silent, and remains silent, so long as it is not proclaimed boldly within the church; the church is nothing but a repressive apparatus of other political and cultural forces if it is not the platform for radical proclamation. Nietzsche's madman had no receptive audience in the streets, and even if the churches he entered were largely empty, thinking God anew there changed and continues to change the world. Our radical insurrections, even and often from small communities of faith, tiled within gothic buildings or in worship occurring in living rooms and bars and malls, may seem insignificant if we answer to the nihilistic lure of orthodoxy which demands anonymity, consumption, and mass appeal to be deemed relevant and important.

As a language-event, we preachers may feel as if we are only preparing the way. As an apocalyptic faith, as a hopeful faith, we are always preaching in the Now that is not-yet. Leading others to embody the crucifixion, to live the death of God, is to realize that an apocalyptic faith must always be not-yet. We are only seeds being planted for the time being. No voting pattern, no political situation, will ever measure up to the actual New, the apocalypse always beyond our grasp. We are called in our preaching to shift mimetic desire for more capital that sustains our political situation into a more genuine imitation of Christ: incarnating, parabolically reversing, healing, perishing, descending, and resurrecting.

Reversal is indicative of all truly radical preaching, as Jesus' parables indicate a radical reversal and Jeremiah Wright's most famous sermons enact transformational reversals, often by simply setting the table of the sanctuary with language to allow the reversals latent in the Bible to simply speak for themselves.[36]

Reversal sometimes takes the form of expressing the "ambiguous lack" which is the consequence of genuine theological practice, and boldly proclaiming the Good News, even when its implications are uncomfortable, disturbing, and point us toward a paradoxical state of affairs, where we are held to account to a challenge that will always just be beyond the grasp of our language and experience.[37] The radical reversal of preaching also takes the form of admitting the awkwardness of trying to live an authentically radical Christian life in twenty-first century America; realizing that even while speaking in the church, which is where radicals must speak if they are radical, the church's leadership wants nothing to do with theological radicalism. For example, my own denomination's workbook for Confirmation classes has several interviews with denominational officials; the *very first one* makes a characterization of radical theology and simply dismisses it.[38] To piggyback on Adam Kotsko's exploration of awkwardness in his treatise on the subject, being a radical Christian can and will lead to awkwardness in our everyday goings-on. Radical preaching embodies and articulates this awkwardness, "the common sense notion of awkwardness as a disturbance in the social fabric," and leads us to embrace our awkwardness "toward something like utopia," preaching the Kingdom of God.[39]

Radical preaching is always a reversal of course, may not always be theologically consistent especially given the variety of contexts in which radicalism may speak, but its authentic reversal is always present, even if the reversal is simply claiming a new language or new way of speaking from and for the theological, ecclesiastical, and social location of radicalism.[40] As I preach later in this volume, we no longer proclaim a Pentecost faith but a Pentecosting faith. And just as Godhead is perpetually changing, so too must our Pentecosting thinking, institutions, and apocalyptic hopefulness.

To these ends, Preaching is never one single practice or a

limited set of practices; this volume is meant to be helpful to preacher, seminarian, and Christian searching for ways to express and think about this Pentecosting for themselves. One common criticism of radical theology is that it is wrapped up in a very narrow system of thinking that is too exclusive or exclusivistic; ironically, this charge comes from those whose religiously exclusionary doctrines are quite inventive. To the contrary, radical theology invites more radical thinking. Radical theologians should expect, in fact, hope, for new radical thinking that resists and transcends our own.

*

The pages that follow present a year in the life of a radical Christian preacher, or at least someone attempting to develop a radical homiletic. The sermons loosely follow the schedule of the Revised Common Lectionary. This is not a complete picture of the Revised Common Lectionary, but snippets of the best sermons through a single year of preaching in a congregation.

Sermon collections from clergy who are not pastors of "major" congregations or famous theologians are today a rare occasion. Many of our greatest theologians' best work occurred in their sermons: Jonathan Edwards, Karl Barth, and Paul Tillich come to mind immediately. This collection is meant to be a testament to the serious theological work that may be done from the pulpit, and also as a bit of a condemnation that the theology often performed in the "academy" fails to answer the questions of the larger community of believers by avoiding public wrestling with our primary theological text, the Bible.

In fact, it is perhaps the twentieth century's most forgotten preacher, Joseph Fort Newton, whose 1919 sermon collection, *Sermons and Lectures*, inspired this collection. *Sermons and Lectures* captures a young Newton, before he became particularly famous, in one year of his preaching life from 1912—1913 , entrenched in the particularities of his local congregation. The progression of sermons in this year includes some occasional academic lectures, including one titled "Nietzsche: Apostle of Anti-Christ," in which he concludes, long before critical scholarship on Nietzsche had been developed and widely published, that "Christ is the true Superman ... He will make supermen of us if we let Him have His way with us—let us follow Him!"[41] Newton understood his audience to be beyond the local church, as he understood his ministry to be beyond the local church. In this collection of sermons, I am, like Joseph Fort Newton, attempting to be a public intellectual whose primary audience is the church.

To these ends, I intend this sermon collection to be useful to preachers searching for ideas and tools for ministry and also to those who enjoy reading sermons. More importantly, however, these sermons as a unified whole represent a *theological work*, and a *theologian at work*, a theologian attempting to communicate the radical message of the death of God on the cross to a local ecclesiastical body. The homiletic space allowed by the congregation is a theology studio. The theology at work here is, I hope, seen as being playful and liberal with its ideas while it takes the source text of scripture and its audience very seriously.

My sources for preaching always include SAMUEL, the United Church of Christ's lectionary preaching resource; Richard Swanson's *Provoking the Gospel* series; and the online Girardian Commentary on the Lectionary.[42] Where I have directly used these or other sources they are cited, though these commentaries are part of the background tapestry for these sermons. It is my hope that you will act as a pirate with my writing and my own piracy, and use these sermons and ideas liberally with your own.

There are simply too many people to acknowledge for their help in preparing these texts. These sermons were mostly preached to the community at Zion "Goshert's" UCC (Lebanon, Pennsylvania), and some of them, in draft form, presented as drafts to the online blogging community of *An und für sich*.[43]

Some of these sermons were also delivered at Grace UCC, Richland, Pennsylvania; The Community Church of Mountain Lakes, New Jersey; the UCC Home in Annville, PA; and St. Paul's UCC in Dallastown, PA. One of the sermons collected here was workshopped at a preaching retreat sponsored by The Beatitudes Society. The late Gabriel Vahanian wrote an interesting critique of two of the sermons presented here, as he was present for them; I also had helpful feedback from Jeffrey Robbins and Noëlle Vahanian. I also thank Tom Altizer and Peter Rollins for their feedback and their contributions to the project. My former students at Lebanon Valley College, Lexington Theological Seminary, Lancaster Theological Seminary, Harrisburg Area Community College, and Penn State York are very often my conversation partners for many of the theological conversations that are behind these sermons. I thank John Hunt Publishing and especially the folks at Christian Alternative and editor Trevor Greenfield for supporting this project. Special thanks for the support of my current congregation, St. Paul's UCC, Dallastown, Pennsylvania, and the church's secretary, Chris Raffensberger

And finally, I wish to thank, of course, my family—Traci, Christian, Annaliese, and Scarlett. The exigency of radical theology and radical preaching is that a future church will be possible.

Christopher D. Rodkey
Feast of St. Thomas Aquinas
January 28, 2013
Dallastown, Pennsylvania

The Seasons of Advent and Christmas

The Jokulhaups

Matthew 24:36-44 (Advent 1)

Today is the first Sunday of Advent, which is the first Sunday of the Christian Year. Advent is typically a time of preparation for the coming of Jesus as a baby in the manger. This is also the first Sunday of the cycle of Bible readings that we will follow in church for the next year, which will be primarily worked through the Gospel of Matthew. Last year we spent almost all year in the Gospel of Luke, and now we enter into the Gospel of Matthew.

In contrast to our Christmas preparations, preparing for Jesus' arrival in a manger as his *First* Coming, the teaching of Jesus that comes to us this week finds Jesus telling his disciples how to be on guard for the *Second* Coming, of his entrance into the world. Jesus famously says that he will come like a thief in the night, and take everyone by surprise. But he also indicates that things will be so different in the Kingdom that he is bringing about that it will be like a flood that washes everything away and the world will begin anew.

This image makes me think of the role-playing game called "Magic: The Gathering," do any of you remember that game? It's apparently still played; in fact, I was writing on my laptop at a local coffee shop about a month ago, and two young men came and sat down at the table next to me and began playing Magic: The Gathering, which surprised me a little because I hadn't seen anyone play it in a while. If you haven't ever seen the game, it's kind of like the game Dungeons and Dragons, except you play the game with cards. That's the only thing I can really explain in a brief way about it.[1]

That said, Magic: The Gathering is a very complicated game and different cards have different magical powers in the game. And some of the cards are scarce and particularly powerful, which makes them actually kind of valuable. Some of the cards can sell for hundreds of dollars, and the annual tournament for the game usually has a $1 million grand prize. So it's a pretty serious endeavor.

Anyway, my brother and I used to play this game late at night when we were in high school. One of my favorite cards was called the "Jokulhaups."[2] It's a big flood, which is why it reminded me of this Bible reading, but what this card did in the game was that it wiped out the playing field. So, just as my brother would get his big guns out in the game, I would throw down this card, which would destroy everything he had worked for in the game, and then I would systematically beat him with the playing cards in my hands.

As we played the game, sometimes my brother would ask me to take the card out of my playing cards because he felt it gave me an unfair advantage and that he would almost always lose the game because of it. But when we played with the card in my deck, my brother would be more patient in the game and wait in anticipation for me to throw down this card, which I never would until the time was just right.

So what does this have to do with Jesus? Jesus' teaching in our scripture reading today teaches that we should live in a manner that we are found faithful if Jesus were to show up again. We should live in anticipation of an event so cataclysmic that we might not even realize it going on around us. Now, I'm not saying we should look for signs of Jesus in natural disaster, although some Christians do this, but Jesus is instructing us to be on guard. No one knows the day, nor the hour. We don't need to worry ourselves with figuring this all out. We just need to be ready.

Last week (The Reign of Christ, Year C)[3] we heard the story of Jesus blessing the criminal on the cross before he died, saying that the criminal will join him in paradise. This gives us a clue about what kind of *wiping of the slate* that God has in mind, namely, that the world order is going to be turned completely upside down, topsy-turvy. The last will be first, and the first will be last. The peacemakers, and the meek, and the poor will be blessed. Those who hold religious authority will be exposed to really having none. And those who claim to possess special knowledge and have visions about the end of the world are not only liars, but their knowledge is not of God. In Jesus' vision for the coming New Creation, there is a great *radical reversal* that we can only begin to understand now.

And this is Jesus' point. We aren't meant to know all of this information now, and that's just fine. So we should not busy ourselves with the specifics but simply be faithful and prepare the way.

*

This is also the story of Jesus' entrance into the world in the first place, as a baby in a manger. The prophets foretold it, the stargazing wise men from the East recognized it, and the virgin secretly prepared the way for Christ's coming into the world. God prepared his people and his earth for *just the right moment* for Jesus to come, and Jesus came in a way few would expect and even fewer would truly accept, in a smelly barn to teenage parents, and then in hiding as children were being slaughtered all around them. This is not how we would expect God to shatter Godself into human history. But this is what we believe, namely, that God works in absurd ways that might make sense in hindsight but rarely make sense in the present moment.

The virgin carrying a baby in the weeks leading up to the birth of Jesus holds all of God's plans, cradled in the waters of a womb, being nurtured by the warmth of her interiority. We should never lose sight of the scandal of this moment in history, and the complete *offense* these ideas would have been for everyone living around Mary.

Within, inside, of this teenage girl is the most cataclysmic event of history, the shattering of Godself into the world. No one, and perhaps not even Mary, could even know just how world-changing the coming of this baby would be. But we now know that the entrance of Jesus into the world came much like Jesus said he will come again: like a flood starting everything new.

So we enter into this season of Advent, this season of preparation for Christmas, with the image of the flood. This image of the Jokulhaups. The water is breaking. And all things that come before Christ's entrance into our lives are destroyed and we may begin anew.

He Touched Me at the Airport

Matthew 3:1-12 (Advent 2)

In November, 2010, the U.S. Transportation Security Administration introduced new security measures at airports, which included the so-called "full-body imaging" technology scans and new policies for "pat-downs" by TSA officials on travelers. A traveler in San Diego refused to be scanned and touched, which resulted in his expulsion from the airport, a civil suit, and a fine. A public outcry followed from the conservative media, focusing upon privacy rights and their heteronormative discomfort with "being touched" at an airport.

As many of you know I recently took an airplane from Harrisburg to a conference and returned to Harrisburg. Amid all of the talk about new airport security, all of the security was not in my opinion invasive. My flight arrived home early, and it was a beautiful autumn day, so I decided to wait for my wife to pick me up outside of the terminal's baggage claim area. If you've ever spent any amount of time at an airport, and have gotten past the aggravation that often comes with being in an airport for an extended amount of time, you know that it can be interesting to watch people coming and going. So I decided to sit down and watch the people coming out of the airport.

If you've been to an airport in the last decade you also know that no one is allowed to park at the entrance to an airport anymore, and there is usually one police car stationed at Harrisburg International Airport to deter people from parking. But when I sat down to watch the people coming and going, I found it odd that there were two police cars there, one parked right where the cars come into the terminal, as if to scare people from parking for an extended amount of time, but the other was behind a truck parked at the very end of the baggage claim area.

The police car wasn't trying to get rid of the truck, it was clear that the truck was supposed to be there, the truck driver was casually talking to the police officer. The police officer was there providing security for whatever was coming or going out of the truck.

Eventually, out of the very last door of the pick-up area came several men pulling and pushing three large carts of pay-phones out of the airport. Each cart had 15 or 20 pay-phones on them. I began to wonder whether there were any pay-phones left in the airport!

Have you ever wondered: will we have to explain to children what pay-phones are, or *were*, in the near future? We can probably think of other things that were once an important part of our household or our culture that are similarly disappearing— I think of the 8-track cassette, for example. The wristwatch will be next—very few young people wear wristwatches because they get their time off of phones or other devices. Fax machines and CB radios will likely follow the pay-phone into the graveyard.

At the same time, I never imagined that the pay-phone would ever go away. As I was watching the pay-phones being taken away from the airport, I kept thinking how much the pay-phone has been a fixture in our culture. If you've ever watched the television show, *Dr. Who*, you know that the Doctor travels through time through a time machine disguised as a British Police phone-booth called a Tardis. So popular was the television show, *Dr. Who*, that a band called The KLF wrote (if you're familiar, I employ the word "wrote" liberally) a song in praise of the time-traveling phone booth, which was a #1 hit in 1988 called "Doctorin' the Tardis."[1] Watching the phone booths being taken away, I wondered, too, isn't the phone booth where Superman changed into his superhero costume in the comic books?

*

The disappearance of the phone booth represents change. And the appearance of John the Baptist on the scene represents change. They are symbols of change. The Bible tells us that John the Baptist began a religious cult in the wilderness. The word "cult" is the most fitting term to use for what he was doing: John began a new religious practice with followers who separated themselves from the rest of the culture.

The image that we get from the Bible of John the Baptist was a kind of rough figure: he wore a shirt of camel hair, lived on a diet of locusts and honey, and we should be clear that when the Bible says that he wore "a leather belt around his waist," the Greek word here is, quite literally, "thong." So the image we have here is not exactly the kind of guest preacher invited to speak at the Crystal Cathedral. Now, even while this crazy guy was out in the wilderness, lots of people were going out to him to be baptized, to be cleansed of the past and to be immersed into something new.

As you can imagine, those with the religious and social power in the Temple in Jerusalem took notice, and the religious conservatives went out to question John the Baptist. When John the Baptist calls them all a "Brood of Vipers," he's not just insulting them, he's swearing at them, more or less saying "Your mamma's a snake!" We should keep this in mind with the images we have of the snake in the Book of Genesis—snakes are vile creatures condemned to slither the earth and eat dirt.[2] Even though we might not be able to really hear that this is swearing with our modern ears, we can probably imagine that going into a bar on Saint Patrick's day and telling an Irishman that his mother's a snake might not fall on deaf ears.

John the Baptist doesn't stop there, he tells the fundamentalists that their authority is wrapped up in their racial ancestry to Abraham, but now the root of the genealogical tree is about to be axed down. He says, "every tree that does not bear good fruit is to be cut down and thrown to the *fire*." This is not just an insult to the Temple or the fundamentalists who act as henchmen for the priests, but John the Baptist is insulting the spiritual authority that all Jews claim to have, including himself as a Jew, that their race is chosen by God. John is not denying that they are chosen by God, but he is claiming that they have done nothing to show anything good for it.

"I baptize you with water for repentance," he concludes, "but one who is more powerful than me is coming after me ... He will baptize you with the Holy Spirit and *fire*." John the Baptist uses the word "fire" three times here. Fire is a symbol of change. Fire destroys things. Fire keeps us warm. As a chemical reaction, fire is pure change. We light candles in churches for many reasons, but one of them is that the ancient Persians and some ancient Greeks believed that God can be known to us through fire.

Fire is a symbol of *change*: it is a chemical reaction that is perpetually in motion. Similarly, John the Baptist represents change, he says that he is not the messiah but the one who is coming, Jesus, is the messiah. The change that John the Baptist is preaching is a temporal change, it is understood that this change will again change: the change is *temporary*, provisional. John baptizing the Jews coming from all directions is all about change, just as the ritual of baptism is all about change. The river where people were baptized is also a symbol of *change*; the philosopher Heraclitus, who believed that fire is the basic element upon which the whole world is built, also famously said, "You never step into the same river twice."[3] Rivers and waters are always changing. John swearing and insulting the religious authorities signifies a change. We might say sometimes that "change is in the air," but here, change is in the fire, and change is in the water, too.

But we also know that fire is especially dangerous. If you've ever had a fire in the house you know how dangerous it can often be, and how destructive it can be, and the changes it brings are not always good. Our military men in World War II often tell the stories of the smell that they would experience as they came to a concentration camp, the smell of death, the stench of incinerated flesh. We remember watching the fires of the World Trade Center burning for days after September 11, 2001. When we imagine John's image of separating the wheat from the chaff with fire, we can also imagine the ashes in the breeze rising from these catastrophic events. When we get frustrated in airport security lines we immediately think of the smoke coming out of lower Manhattan and then we remember why we have gone through so many changes in our culture in the past ten years.

What John represented was not simply change, but a *genuine threat*, a threat to the Temple, to society, and to everything that Jews held dear. John the Baptist, and his preaching about the coming of Jesus, was not necessarily Good News to everyone who heard it. These words were fearful. These were words that genuinely threatened those with power and authority, and those who wanted to apprehend or stop the change. And we should always remember that John the Baptist was beheaded for preaching change.

*

So much of our political and social discourse over the last two or three years has been about "change you can believe in" (from President Barack Obama). The problem with "change that we can believe in" is that if you need to make a call and you have no payphones around, the change is really meaningless, let alone useless. The kind of change John the Baptist is talking about is a complete topsy-turvy revolution, where the last is first and the first is last. It's not about the end of the world but about the Alpha and the Omega, the beginning and the end: beginning and ending with Jesus. *It is a change we could not possibly believe, because it is beyond belief.*

So many of us want change to happen around us, or with us,

or in us, but too often the change we seek is just one small step to what and where God is really calling us to go. And if the voice in the wilderness is calling for us to change in ways beyond belief, are we really listening?

Queer Accusation!

Isaiah 35:1-10; James 5:7-10; Matthew 11:2-11 (Advent 3)

Last week I talked about John the Baptist and how he called those in the Temple a "Brood of Vipers" which is John the Baptist's swearing. We hear some more swearing in this week's Bible reading, but you have to look very closely and turn off our modern ears to hear it.

Our Bible reading opens with John the Baptist in prison. Here we have the first time that someone in the story recognizes Jesus as the Messiah, although this is implied in the story. John the Baptist apparently has his *own* disciples, separate from Jesus' disciples, and John sends his disciples to investigate Jesus and his ministry. They want to know, "Are you the Messiah?" Jesus' answer is "Go and tell John the Baptist about my healing: the blind receive sight, the lame walk, and the lepers are cleansed, the deaf hear, the dead are raised, and the poor now have hope."

So Jesus doesn't really answer the question, but this is all code language between John the Baptist and Jesus. They both know and understand that if Jesus were to say, "why, yes, I am the Messiah," and hand over a business card that says, *Jesus, Certified Messiah*, we might have a clear sign that he would *not* be the messiah, since so many others during this time bragged to be a messiah. Instead, Jesus is saying, look around at what is happening; the world order is going into a *great reversal*: the sick are *now* healthy. The poor *now* have hope. Those in power are *now* trembling with fear." But this also means that they are all *now* living in dangerous times. John the Baptist is in jail, rejected by his own people, waiting to be beheaded. Jesus, we all know, will be executed later.

Then Jesus says something extraordinary: "blessed is anyone who takes no offense at me." We should remember that this episode occurs at the beginning of Jesus' ministry, and Jesus was not yet on the radar screens of anyone with any power, he only had a small movement of twelve disciples. Was Jesus predicting that he would offend people? Why would anyone be offended?

This is a question I have been wrestling with over the past week. My wife and I found out that some students at the nearby teaching hospital were doing free ultrasounds as part of their training, so we volunteered to get a free 3-D ultrasound on Tuesday. As we were watching the ultrasound image of a baby still in preparation to enter the world emerge out of the dark monitor connected to all of these wires that the nursing student was navigating, it suddenly occurred to me that it was this very week a year ago that we lost a baby to miscarriage. This memory suddenly hit me like a ton of bricks, while watching this murky image of a little, healthy baby just waiting until her right time to come out.

That evening we dropped our son off at his grandmother's house and we left to go to dinner with a couple with whom we had been looking forward to getting together for some time. As we were driving to the diner, my telephone rang. They weren't going to make it because they had just had a miscarriage, the wife was at the hospital. We were only a handful of people who knew that they were pregnant.

What made Advent so difficult for my wife and I last year was losing a child in the middle of a season preparing for a miraculous birth, which is then met with the tension of hundreds and hundreds of babies being slaughtered in Bethlehem following the death of Jesus. And now we know that two of our friends are experiencing the same tragedy right now, as do many young couples at this time of year.

What I'm painting is this: could it be that when Jesus is saying, "I hope no one is offended by me," the offense is not about anything Jesus is doing, or at least not yet. Jesus is instead saying, *blessed is the one who resents me for being me, who I am,* that is, the lone survivor of the slaughter of all of those babies who died in the Slaughter of the Holy Innocents. *Jesus' survival alone is offensive*, and his very presence implies that someone resented him for it. The locals knew he survived the slaughter of children by Herod's order, and they knew that their children did not.

But then there's this other side of it, that men of Jesus' age who were not married were not trusted by the culture. We don't know whether most of the disciples were married or not, but if they were, they left their homes pretty quickly to follow Jesus. John the Baptist was seen as being weird; running around in a thong; hanging out 'down by the river';[1] eating bugs; and *most importantly, unmarried*. And then his cousin, Jesus, started doing magic tricks and healing people around Capernaum, which was a hotspot for wealthy people to solicit faith healers. Clearly, the two of them were not considered polite company.

*

So then Jesus began to speak about John the Baptist, saying that John the Baptist is not some hippie hanging out in a commune but a rough guy, he's not a weed easily shaken by the wind, and he's not some pansy wearing nice, soft clothes. The word in Greek used here to describe the clothes is "malakos," soft, but more than soft, effeminate. Clothing that is "malakos" is dainty, fancy, women's clothes.

Perhaps it was Jesus who was accused of being gay by some of the townsfolk. All of the other boys his age in his hometown were killed, and with an abundance of women his age from which to choose a wife, he chose none. And then he became associated with the John the Baptist, also single, wearing a thong down by the river. So Jesus throws an insult back to those who make fun of John the Baptist, against those who make rash accusations of Jesus and John. While invoking the name of the thong-wearing John the Baptist, Jesus is saying that *the ones who make fun of John and Jesus for being queer are the real queers.* They sit in their temples and posh buildings wearing robes—and we should remember that a robe is really a dress, just like I wear on Sundays—and *they* accuse Jesus and John of being *strange*? And then, to make matters worse, after calling those in charge a bunch of queers, Jesus then quotes scripture, words from the prophets of the Old Testament. He concludes by saying, "Verily I say to you, no prophet has yet to arise greater than John the Baptist," you might say he dresses like a girl, but he is a true prophet.

What are we to make of all of this? Jesus makes a claim attacking the masculinity of his accusers, a notion that I find to be a little problematic in the eyes of our modern world, where we understand that it's not polite to call someone a queer or for a kid to tease another kid for being gay on the playground. Clearly, the point is *not* that Jesus makes bullying or name-calling permissible. What I think all of this points to, is that there is a tremendous *reversal of the social order* going on where these unmarried men, one of which is really strange hanging out in the wilderness, are the true messengers of God whereas the temple priests are seen as the enemy. And Jesus' words cuts to the chase: "Why are they calling us strange when they're the ones wearing women's clothing?" It's kind of like, if you can imagine, going back into the 1940s and accusing a priest or a minister of being a pedophile. That would have been unthinkable decades ago, and then it became a joke that priests are pedophiles. And now we know the truth: that many pedophiles entered the ministry because it gave them cover to get away with it.

Beyond this, Jesus' accusation to those in power, wearing women's clothing, is a charge of *decadence*, that they live the high life while everyone else suffers. And the point of the story is that Jesus is healing all sorts of people while they sit in their comfortable homes. But the point *isn't* just that those in power are hypocrites, but more poignantly, those in power are completely removed from the ground where people actually *live* and *suffer*—and this is not just where John the Baptist and Jesus are, serving the people by giving hope, offering ritual, preaching, and healing, but it is on the ground, with the people, *with humanity*, where God *is*, with the suffering servants. *God is on the ground*, and God is with us; in fact, we know that the name that Mary is instructed to give to Jesus is Emmanuel, which means "God-with-us."

*

So much of our Christmas celebration is giving gifts and sharing family time. Even though the commercialization of Christmas makes many of us uncomfortable, but I think most of us can reconcile that our huge celebration of Christmas is an extension of the religious holiday of Christmas. We like the image of Jesus being born to teenage parents. We like the images of animals around the baby. We put nativity displays everywhere.

We forget that *this baby is God*, and this is not only God who came to us in a smelly, dirty barn amidst the violence of slaughtered children in his hometown, and it is not just that Jesus himself as a baby became a refugee, and illegal immigrant on the run from the law, but *the real scandal is that God came into the world at all*. And he came not into the world to live among the ruling class or to be a leader in the religious institutions but to show us that this God is *down-to-earth*, because he *came down to earth*; that this God favors those who suffer, and the poor. God *reverses* the course of history by showing that God is very different to those with the very loud voices in the culture, who say that he is or could or should be; and furthermore, this God cares especially for those who have no voice in their own society.

And that this God *unmasks* those who preach hate as liars and hypocrites themselves, but this God known to us as Jesus is a God with us, a God healing us and bringing us to new levels of wholeness and compassion for those often very different from us all, because when we understand that the God who is Emmanuel, God-with-us, died for the sins of the world, this God is not just a *God for just-us*, but a *God for all of us*.

'Christmas' isn't in the Bible?

Jeremiah 31:15; Matthew 2:13-23
(Christmastide 1/Feast of the Holy Innocents)

The Story of the Slaughter of the Holy Innocents is not a story that we like to tell, and it's in the Bible as a reminder to those of us celebrating the twelve days of Christmas in contemporary times to acknowledge the violence and horror of Christmas.

The complete Christmas story is one that is not for those with a weak stomach. The details disclose a story not really suitable for children's books. The main idea of the story is that the king murdered hundreds, if not thousands of babies of a people already heavily burdened and oppressed. In the Bible we hear the shrieking of Rachel crying over her children, who were murdered by the orders of a tyrannical ruler afraid of a little baby. We recall that only a century and a half before, Jewish children were killed by their oppressors if the boys were found to have been circumcised, and part of the punishment was that the dead baby was to be hung around the mother's neck. This memory is in the back of everyone's mind as a terrible event long in the past, but the present has become a lot worse. Jesus' coming into the world is not yet Good News for anyone; in fact it's a whole lot of bad news. Now the messiah comes and the Christmas story, with all the gifts and joy, gets real, real fast.

And we should recall that an act this wretched, this infanticide of all of these babies, is not just something that happened and then it was simply over. The babies would have been buried by Jewish custom. If you know anyone who has lost a child you know that they often have an open wound that never completely heals; sometimes that wound offers some hope but it is an overwhelming pain. The pain can feel like a mark on them for the rest of their lives, like an 'X': something that has crossed out a piece of their souls. In our story, it's not just one grieving family, but many; in fact, it's a whole region of babies killed.

How are we to find meaning in this story today? I have two points, and they're both about contradictions and reversals in this story. My first point is one I just mentioned, that in this story we find a tremendous contradiction regarding the joy of Christmas. Perhaps this story underscores that the Christmas that is celebrated in our culture is not only a gross misinterpretation of the Christian or Biblical notion of Christmas, but beyond this our secular and deeply pagan celebrations of Christmas are a blasphemy to anything authentically Christian as reflected in the Bible.

You can call me a "scrooge" or a "grinch," but I think you all know what I'm talking about. It's a historical fact that the Pilgrims who settled Massachusetts Bay Colony, who are our spiritual forebears in the United Church of Christ, actually outlawed Christmas from being celebrated outside of the church and outside of the home. They felt that if Christmas was left to its own devices that the meaning of the holiday would be diminished and dissolved by a spiritually sick culture. The banning of Christmas for years was used as the prime example of how the Puritans went too far with their laws, but I think we can all see that they had a point.

Often those trying to be authentically Christian during Christmas miss the point, and here's an example. I am sure you've heard people complain and bemoan the term "X-Mas," as an intentional way of taking Christ out of Christmas. The thing a lot of people don't understand is that the letter "X," the Greek letter Chi, has always been a symbol of Christ, and in fact was an early symbol used in the church even when Christians met in secret. Christians have used the term "X-Mas" for centuries. In fact, the heterodox and subversive use of the term "X-Mas" may even be *less offensive* to the Bible and what's going on in the scriptures than what we call "Christmas."

So, beyond the contradiction between what Christmas is and how we often celebrate it, we secondly have a contradiction between forces of power in the Bible story. The king will do *anything* to get rid of Jesus. He tried tricking the Wise Men, but they figured him out and *they tricked him.* Jesus' coming into the world, his Advent, is not just a threat to this particular ruler, King Herod, but is a threat to all rulers. Herod knows he must not only react, and react as swiftly and violently as possible, but he has to make a good show of his efforts: if Rome were to discover that the messiah arrived on Herod's watch, it would be Herod's head. And even beyond this, Herod seems to know and understand that this little baby, born to refugee parents, contradicted the entire idea of political power, that Jesus genuinely threatened a *reversal* of the entire institution of the ruling political forces.

And to go even further: this little Baby is so *subversive* that he is not only the King of Kings, but Kings will pass away and die off, empires will fall, holocausts will happen because of the evil hearts of men and their rulers, and yet Jesus stands as the one constant and consistent Word of God, brought forth and *kenotically poured out* from the spoken words of God at Creation and judge of the living and the dead at the end of time. This little baby represented a radical reversal of everything anyone with power could possibly know, and Herod responded with the most radically vile and extreme measure that he could comprehend, that is, to slaughter all of the male children of an entire town.

*

We stand today, some 2,000 years or so later, after these babies were all buried, still reeling in the joy of the commercial Christmas, far removed from the big "X" placed upon the lives of hundreds, if not thousands, of women and their families on this day of terror and unconceivable loss. Like women who have suffered a pregnancy loss, as one out of every three women in the

U.S. today have, there is no grave left to go for mourning. No memorial to remember for us to acknowledge when we are gone. Just a big "X" that is experienced universally all over the place.

And yet we are called by God to respond to this profound sense of loss, which is increasingly difficult to do while Christmas has been hijacked to become something that is not Christmas. We are called to proclaim the Jesus who comes as a baby in the manger, a Jesus who threatens the power of politicians and dictatorships. We proclaim a Jesus who is the *opposite*, a reversal, of the Christ of popular Christianity and its secular holiday of Christmas, but the "X" of "X-Mas," who crosses out the false messiahs and false Christs presented to us every day in the form of ideologies, substance abuse, and the exploitation and commodification of our bodies, especially the bodies of children.

The question of us is whether we are willing to pay the cost of discipleship today and stand up for Jesus? Are we willing to let the words of the Bible reside comfortably *in* the book of the Bible, or let the words of a God who is still speaking *annunciate* through us and in us in this new day and in our new year? Does Jesus come to us as a neatly-packaged gift box that is easily contained, or as a baby born in the messiness of human birth amidst a tremendous reality of danger and violence? Are we willing to experience a profound sense of loss to come into the new life that Christ affords? While thousands of people return to the stores to return gifts they don't want in these days following the First Day of Christmas, the question demanded to us is whether we are ready to turn in our old selves to become a new and beautiful New Creation?

Creationism is Atheism

Genesis 1:1-2:3; Ephesians 1:3-14; John 1:1-18
(Christmastide 2)

The opening of the Gospel of John indicates a new beginning, as it is a kind of creation story: *In the beginning was the Word and the Word was with God.* There is much we could unpack with these words, but I want to get down to the basics of what this language really means, which, at bottom is saying that before Genesis 1, before the beginning of the world, Jesus, as the son of God, was the conduit through which all creation came from. In other words, God's first creation was Jesus, as the first Word spoken by God, and through this first Word all other words came, as God spoke the universe into creation.

So what does it mean to say that the world is created *through* Jesus Christ? What does it mean to say that Jesus' fingerprints are all over everything in the world? Traditionally, the answer to this question is that God created the world for the purpose of sending his son into it to save the world. For me, this is a deeply unsatisfying answer, because it seems to me that the whole ordeal of the universe itself would be an unnecessary exercise unless God is just really plain bored. Or boring, for that matter.

But Jesus' touch on everything, including all people, is a pervasive reminder to us that we are all siblings of the great family of humanity and the single divine paternity of God. It is also a reminder that it is wrong to say that God is more present in certain parts of the world and with certain people, than with others. People can reject God and people may do ungodly things, but this is not to say that God abandons individuals or that God is absent from evil situations. We believe that God's grace is so powerful and interwoven with all things that exist that God is never really absent so long as we continue to exist.

46

Much of the debates in our culture about creation—whether it should be taught in schools and so forth—we all know to be petty arguments that place a limitation upon God as not really being *present* in the *present*, but instead these arguments render God to be a dead relic of the past. In fact, I would go so far as to say that when we argue to impose the Biblical account of Creationism upon public schools, in the same way people talk about prayer in schools and the ten commandments in court-houses, we imply for ourselves a *deep atheism* that reflects a lack of belief in a God who is still creating, still speaking creation, and still offering grace to sinners in a world that is inherently broken. These kinds of arguments are atheistic in that they reflect a lack of faith in a God who still exists vibrantly in our communities and in our lives—that the greatest acts of God are not only in the past, but they ceased being extraordinary at the very moment of creation.

If we claim to believe in Jesus as "the Word," we then believe that the first act of God's creation was creating a plan for our salvation, a giving of himself that is so radically self-subverting that God himself would sacrifice himself on the cross for the sake of the same humanity that was created through the same Word. The Words of creation are slaughtered on the cross as a culmi-nation of God's first acts of creation. God's death on the cross reflects a *weakness* of God, a weakness and humility that calls us forth to be disciples of this weakness, ministering to those who are weak and downtrodden, those who are dying and those who are sick and impoverished.

But in addition to our ministry to others, we are called to be, or to become, creative and creating beings ourselves. Often when we think of our own kind of creation, we think of procreation, having children, or of making art: activities which pull the essence of ourselves into something concrete and tangible in the world. But as we are created in God's image we also share Godly creativity, meaning that we all participate in a universal creative spirit that thrives off of the connectedness of ourselves to others and to all of creation, that we are all saturated as parts of this huge and beautiful web of creation.

This webbing that connects us all is Christ; it is now up to us to make this web of Christ known to ourselves and everyone around us. We enact this webbing through acts of justice, acts of charity, and acts of mercy, but it is done in simple ways of offering warmth and hospitality to others, encouraging our young people to walk in the faith, and to pray for ourselves and each other. Some of us do this through evangelism, inviting others to church or encouraging them in their faith journeys in other churches, and some of us do it through ritual.

The web of Christ all around us is not an argument to be won or lost, because when we begin arguing about the truth or the politics of the "truth" we in turn diminish God in our midst and our faith can become dissolved into a movement against certain things, instead of building relationships and relationalities. And we know that these kinds of arguments lead many away from the faith, because so often Christianity, when it enforces beliefs upon others, is really atheistic, because it has ceased to have faith in the web of Christ that is all around us, and has always been around us, and requires us to keep spinning and netting in new brothers and sisters in faith. We can only reach out to others by showing how strong the mystical tie is between us all that unites us.

This is our Good News in this New Year, which is a secular time of new beginnings and resolutions, that we are to build ourselves spiritually into something new and strong and focus on our faith in Christ by making this faith real all around us, connecting ourselves to each other. It is in our new commitment to Christ that God is made actual in the hidden spaces between and around us, so that we might continue this moment of Christmas, when the Word is made flesh, within our own flesh through the whole year.

The Season of Epiphany

Where Cloves Come From

Isaiah 42:1-9, Matthew 3:13-17
(The Baptism of the Lord)

When we hear the story of the baptism of Jesus from Matthew 3, it's hard for us to picture what is happening because of the way we do baptisms today. I've been to baptisms in rivers and streams, I've witnessed a baptism happening behind the bars of a maximum-security prison, I myself have baptized babies, toddlers, and adults. I've also seen baptisms done in churches where they have a pool on the stage and the congregation can see into the side of the pool. I've been a member of a church where adults had to take a nine-month class for the privilege of being baptized, and as you know my policy today is that baptism is offered, no questions asked, to anyone that wishes to be baptized, and I do this because this is how the first Gentile was baptized by the apostle Philip in the book of Acts (8:26ff.).

Today's reading from the Bible finds John the Baptist out in the wilderness, smelly and sunburned, baptizing Jews who are looking for a new kind of faith that goes beyond the legalism of those who ran the temple back in Jerusalem. The way Matthew tells the story is that the baptism of Jesus is the first thing that has happened in 30 years that is important to include in the Jesus story; we jump from the three wise men visiting Jesus as a baby to Jesus coming to the riverbanks of the Jordan.

So what happened between the Epiphany and the baptism? There are other texts written during the early days of the church that have some stories of Jesus' baptism; the fact is we don't know. Whatever happened places Jesus as an individual with others who were fed up with how the temple had become a tool and mouthpiece of certain economic and political powers that were seen to be as divorced from authentic Judaism. Jesus travels outside of town, away from the temple, to be part of a fringe group meeting and hoping for something better, but also undergoing a ritual that separated and isolated themselves from the mainstream Jews back in the city.

So Jesus emerges as part of this radical fringe group, and suddenly, John the Baptist recognizes Jesus as the messiah, and tells Jesus that he should be baptizing John, not the other way around. Jesus instead insists that John baptize him, showing that Jesus is not necessarily above all of those other disgruntled radicals who join him at the river but he stands with them. They may be risking their livelihoods and their lives to be there with John in the Jordan River, and Jesus also takes on that risk.

So we should remember that in this instance there was no nine-month baptism class, there was no baptism certificate, there weren't any godparents, and we should remember that John the Baptist didn't wear a robe, he was nearly nude baptizing this other man in the river, spontaneously in the wilderness.

Then, famously, making this baptism even more unusual, the sky tears open above the two of them and the Holy Spirit descends upon them and a voice speaks, "This is my Son, chosen and marked by my love, the delight of my life."

*

Today is the first Sunday that follows the Epiphany; this Sunday is typically called "The Baptism of the Lord." An *epiphany* is when light sparks in the darkness, like when a light bulb goes off in our heads. When we come to a sudden realization or moment of clarity. When I think of my own experience of an "epiphany," I am reminded of when I worked at a grocery store, stocking shelves. When you stock a grocery store you realize just how many different kinds of foods there are and just how strange some of the food can sometimes be. In fact, the night crew at the grocery store would sometimes have money bets on who would eat certain foods they would find in the store, although those foods were usually from the Spanish food aisle, such as canned octopus. I remember seeing for the first time anchovy paste, and wondering not only what you would use this for but who would ever purchase anchovy paste, but I now know that anchovy paste is popularly used in many seafood dishes.

But there were always two items in that grocery store that I remember seeing and having an epiphany over. The first was when I was stocking the spice aisle, which was not a fun aisle to stock because of all of the little jars and it was easy to break things in that aisle. It was one night I discovered ground cloves. Now, I remember learning in school that cloves came from trees, and I knew people that smoked clove cigarettes, but I didn't really know what cloves were for—I know now they're primarily used in Indian food—but I kept looking at the title on the little jar: *ground cloves*. And I kept wondering, "where else do cloves come from, if not the ground?" As I pondered this for a while, it suddenly dawned on me that the word "ground" here meant the cloves *were* ground, and not *from the* ground.

The second time I had this happen was when I was in charge of the baby products aisle, and having never been around babies I had no idea what any of the stuff was in the aisle, other than I had to be careful because those jars of baby food were hard to put on the shelf and were easy to break, and they also expired quickly, so older products had to be regularly moved to the front of the shelf. One day one of the managers completely re-arranged the baby aisle and asked me to make an inventory of all of the new products we would carry that had vacant spots on the shelf, because the store was expanding its baby products. The first time I came to this huge new pegboard it had no products on, but had lots of tags for products we should order.

So I made my list, but I had to stop and think when I got to a product called a "nipple brush." I kind of laughed about it at first, but then I asked myself: why in the world would a nipple need a brush? A few hours later, I walked into the local K-Mart looking for a nipple brush, because I had to know what this was. And then when I saw it, it made sense, it was a tool to clean the rubber nipples for bottle-fed babies.

We have all had these epiphany experiences, when we are confused about something and suddenly the light comes on us, and we say, *"Duh!"*

*

What is going on here in today's scripture reading is that from among the crowds of this radical fringe group arises Jesus, who we know from the Christmas story is the messiah with a very specific plan. The foreign kings recognize his authority; the shepherds, who were outcasts of their society, recognize Jesus; and suddenly the light goes off among this group of people that Jesus is the messiah. We should keep in mind that those Baptists following John in the wilderness would have been seen as a dangerous group of blasphemers and heretics by the mainstream of society. Clearly, we have God working in the fringes of society, far away from the temple and far away from the powers of the temple.

But more importantly it is out of the confusion of different Jewish sects fighting with each other and fighting for a very small piece of political control that Jesus comes up, out of the water, thereby making the baptisms of all of those John had baptized before now meaningful beyond being separatists from the rest of society. In fact, by being separatists they are now in the knowledge that they are to inherit the kingdom of God and to build it for future generations who will be baptized with them, and whose baptisms are made meaningful by the baptism of Jesus.

It's kind of like if you find a piece to a car lying on the road, and this particular piece might not look like anything special to you, but for the car that is broken down on the road three miles past you, the part is essential. But you don't know just how important that piece of the car is until you know what it is for and what it does. Or that using ground cloves could be the essential part of a recipe, whereas if you don't know what it is, the spice is useless.

So it is also with our baptisms. Most of us were probably baptized as children, and some of us long ago. And we believe that baptism is what binds us together as a community, but our baptisms are meaningless if we don't know what to do with it or if it's meaningless to our everyday lives. What we need is the presence of Jesus near us, whether in a friend, or in church, or in a song, or in scripture, to turn the light on for us so we can look back at our past and say, "duh!" Why didn't I live this way before?

We are not always so fortunate to have the clouds tear open with a voice, but what we do have is our faith, our reason, experience, the scriptures, and a whole lot of other disciples in the church to keep us on the journey of baptism, which is a journey of surprises, reversals, overcoming tragedies, and in the end finding an ultimate joy with Christ.

Lord, You have Come to the Lakeshore[1]

Matthew 4:12-23 (Epiphany 3)

In this morning's Bible lesson, Jesus appears more or less out of nowhere at Capernaum "by the sea," which was known to be a place where faith healers hung around, because there were often wealthy people vacationing there. Capernaum was kind of like the regional spa, and there was lots of work for people like Jesus, who was a carpenter, and for fishermen, because of the wealth that the region attracted. Jesus initially appears to the fishermen as just another faith healer, but instead of trying to scam them out of their money by doing a magic trick, he *reverses* their preconceived notions, and instead *preaches*, "Repent, for the kingdom of heaven is near," and suddenly these fishermen just get up and leave.

Two things are indicated as being left behind, their families and their nets. Let me first talk about their nets. All of my years in school and living in cities, I never really learned how to use many tools, which also has to do with my father not being a very handy person, but I am slowly learning some basic things.

On Friday night I put together a small solid wood bookcase, which involved me realizing that I put one piece of pinewood where another should have been, and I ended up having to take the whole thing apart and start over again. Of course, I realized that I had done something wrong just as I was about to finish, and I was thinking to myself, "I'm really getting better at this stuff," and I looked at my tools.

One thing I've learned is that having the right tools makes all the difference and people that work with tools have a particular kind or brand of tools they like, and once you have a good tool, you treasure it. As people that work with tools know, those good working tools become an extension of the person's body, an essential element of the labor that creates a living. You usually try to have the best tools that you can afford.

The Bible tells us that the fishermen left behind their nets. Their nets were their working tools, and they probably invested as much money into those nets as they could, and they just left them behind. But leaving them behind was not just leaving behind their tools, but they also left behind their ability to have a secure livelihood. They would then follow Jesus into towns, into the mountains, and into the desert, and later into death. The disciples were leaving the source of their livelihood: the sea where they had probably grown up and fishing may have been just about all they had ever known. Their nets lay on the ground behind them.

And there stood James and John's father Zebedee, probably of old age and dependent upon his children, mending the nets. The disciples left their families—we don't know if they had wives or children, tradition tells us that they were probably single, but we really don't know. It says something about the way Christians often rail on about "family values" when the beginning of Jesus' ministry begins with men leaving their homes and, if not leaving their wives and children behind, they left behind their elderly father to fend for himself.

I don't think in this world in which we find ourselves today where absences of individuals from their families—fathers and mothers denying their children, people working harder than they had to before to make ends meet, and so on—that the exigent message of our story is that to follow Jesus means that you leave everything and everyone behind. But at the same time we need to recognize that following Jesus is a tremendous inconvenience. In fact, no statistics show this but I honestly think that one reason why young people have generally abandoned the church is that being a Christian is terribly inconvenient to the lifestyles our culture has taught them to be entitled to. It's inconvenient to be a disciple. It's easier to sleep in on Sundays. It's easier to buy a nicer cell phone or a nicer car than sacrifice for charity.

The inconvenience of the Gospel is that following it is *risky*. It is also terribly frightening to many people, when we're concerned about pandemics and sanitation, to share bread that other people have touched around the communion table. It's even more frightening for some to shake other people's hands. It's uncomfortable to do random acts of kindness for others. It's even more counterintuitive to the way our society is to believe that we have a need to say that we're sorry for our sins.

So when Jesus appears on the beach, preaching: "Repent! For the Kingdom of Heaven has come near!" Jesus is speaking into a culture, much like ours, that has become spiritually complacent and lazy, and it is not the priests who respond to Jesus, it is not the elders collecting their social security off of their children's work who respond, and it is not the leaders and the politicians who respond. Who else responds *but the young people* who were probably waiting and just *yearning* for someone to come and preach the truth to them.

Jesus arrives, preaching *repentance* and the closeness of the Kingdom of God—that there is a God, and that God loves us so much that he will forgive us just for the asking—to a group of tough guys working along the banks of the sea, and surprisingly, a few people choose to follow. The others might have nodded their heads, they may have approved or agreed with what Jesus was preaching, but only a few stepped up and made a radical change in their lives and left with Jesus.

And when they left, an *absence* remained to their families. Their tools were no longer being used by their breadwinners. The disciples became less productive members of society in terms of their labor and presence. Sometimes we are called to leave our homes for the purpose of the greater good—be it leaving for school, for work, for adulthood, for military service, or just starting over. But the closeness of the Kingdom of God, as Jesus preached, demands that we move beyond our comfort and our expectations of how our lives are going to turn out. The Kingdom of God does not demand that we destroy our old selves, but that we *reverse and transform* our relationships and *renew* our purpose that God has called for each of us from the beginning of time.

A recent study of church-going Americans asked what American Christians want from their church experience, and Americans responded that what they want out of a church is a faith that "works for them" and teaches them how to live prosperously. It is no wonder that people love the television and radio preachers who preach the Gospel of wealth and the "Chicken Soup for the Soul" that is a feel-good religion. Instead, the Jesus we encounter in the Bible yells at us, screaming, "Repent!" That our lives are more than just about ourselves, but about enacting justice for the poor, turning the social order upside down, and giving hope to those who have none.

The fishermen were not rich, and they gave up what little they had, to begin Jesus' healing ministry, and it is on this point that Jesus launches into the Sermon on the Mount, which will be the topic of next week's sermon, where Jesus famously preaches, "Blessed are the poor, and those who mourn, and those who hunger, and the merciful, and the meek, and the pure in heart, and the peacemakers," and so on.

But we should remember that Jesus appears in Capernaum, by the sea, where many wealthy people hang out and pay faith healers to alleviate their diseases, and when Jesus calls the workers away, he calls them not just as a *healer of diseases* but as a healer of society, and calls them away *for the most important event of human history*. The healing that Jesus offers is not just for small diseases or even life-threatening diseases, but for the mending of a broken world, a spiritually sick world that teaches us to worship ourselves and to seek out our own wealth as the end goal. And Jesus travels directly from the faith healing center of the rich in Capernaum, to the working class fishermen, and then to the poor. As the disciples leave their homes, they are about to completely *reverse* human society, an event that began then and continues now to this day.

The God who is Still Speaking is still calling us by the lakeshore with the same message that was given to those men 2,000 years ago. *We* are not being asked to become absent to our families, but *we* are demanded to make big changes to our lives, and to create absences of influences and forces in our lives, and in society, that create suffering and oppression. *We* are still being called to bless the meek, and the poor, and the poor in spirit, and those who mourn, but so often the religious messages that we hear in our media are mean-spirited, obsessed with the self, and really an elaborate way of patting ourselves on the back.

The questions now upon us are whether *we are really going to respond*, and be present to the real workings of the Spirit in the coming Kingdom of God, or let Jesus' call be a call to an absence, as we turn away from the hard work and tough decisions which Jesus demands?

One theologian calls the meaning of repentance as an engagement with the real world which Jesus demands as being *present in the present*.[2] Often we are absent in the present moment, but Jesus calls us to become mindful of everyone around us, to become *present in the present*. We need to begin to understand that this idea of repentance is not so much about judgment and judging others but it is a gift, perhaps a *present*—a present of being present in the present—in a way that leads us to life *in the present*, into real life, away from *absence* of ourselves and into a love and affinity for all of God's creation and all of God's people.

The Be-Attitudes

Micah 6:1-8; Matthew 5:1-12 (Epiphany 4)

The way the Gospel of Matthew tells this story is that Jesus is born in poverty as an immigrant, displaced from his home country, visited by royalty, by kings from another country and a different religion, then appearing on the banks of the Jordan River with other religious radicals, and then appearing in the spas of Capernaum with the rich, and then to the working class, and then to the poor, to whom he gives his famous Sermon on the Mount, also known as "the Beatitudes." Many of you might have had to memorize these verses of scripture when you were young. I remember that I had to memorize the Beatitudes to enter the fifth grade Sunday School class. And we have heard these words before: blessed are the poor in spirit, and those who mourn, and the meek, and those who hunger for righteousness, and the merciful, and the pure in heart, and the peacemakers, and the persecuted, and so on.

Throughout history these words have often been interpreted, believe it or not, as a justification for the oppression of the poor, or even to legitimize war. The idea is that since Jesus speaks of the Kingdom of God as something coming in the future, it is not the responsibility of everyone else to care for the poor and the widowed and the down-and-out. The words "blessed are the peacemakers" are sometimes even invoked by politicians to demand respect for their war campaigns. But clearly, this is not what is really going on in these verses of the Bible. Instead, Jesus is mapping out his social agenda, which is to *radically reverse* the entire world order. Jesus travels from the rich to the poor and then preaches to the poor, and they listen. Jesus offers hope and meaningfulness to them.

But the heart of what Jesus is *really* saying is about civility on some levels. Did any of you see the news about the walk-out by our State Representatives in Harrisburg this past week?[1] On the internet you can see the whole video, and more or less, one party voted to change the rules that they do not have to allow anyone from the minority party to have representation on any state legislative committee, thereby not only stalling the process of the minority party passing their bills, but instead cutting them out of even having a voice. In essence, one political party has stopped any district who votes for the minority party from having any representation on the legislative committees, which is where the real work of creating laws and state programs happens. The minority party walked out of the meeting, throwing papers and calling the chair of the rules committee names.

We now live in a libelous culture where anyone can say anything about anyone and more or less get away with it. The truth of what is happening doesn't matter but only what perceptions are, is what seems to matter to people. We can label certain people "Democrat," or "Republican," or "independent," or "male" or "female," or "rich" or "poor," but when it comes to Jesus, these labels no longer have any meaning. What Jesus is saying is that the poor should no longer be defined simply by being poor. Those who mourn shall no longer be confined to the chains of mourning. Those who are oppressed in spirit will no longer be understood as only victims of oppression. So often we get labeled as one thing or another, and sometimes these labels are a consequence of good or bad choices we may have made over the years, but Jesus is the game-changer. He, like the majority party in Harrisburg, changes the rules, but instead of limiting voice and representation, Jesus opens the floodgates to God not just for some, and not just for the overly pious, and not just for those who can afford to follow all of the laws, but *now* Jesus offers liberation to those who are truly oppressed and downtrodden.

In other words, Jesus offers a hope that we can live in a world where we can simply *be*. The philosopher Paul Tillich, who was a United Church of Christ theologian, wrote a book called *The Courage to Be*.[2] In the book he argued that what God most wants us to do is to simply be ourselves and be in love with ourselves. This is not to say that we don't have to sometimes change our ways, but that we must simply accept our way of *be-ing* in the world. We can no longer let the labels or titles given to us be a way we are defined, for, as the Bible teaches us, there is neither Jew nor Greek, male or female, slave nor free in Jesus.[3]

In the neighborhood where my mother-in-law lives, there is a house down the block, where, on any evening during the three seasons, the man who lives in that house is outside working on his property. The way he mows the lawn creates perfect diagonal lines in the grass. Every tree and shrub is trimmed and pruned perfectly with straight and round lines. I wouldn't be surprised if every flower has the same number of petals. It's obvious that this man has a deep love for caring for his plants and his yard, but you can also see that it's kind of obsessive—I'm sure you know people who are like this.

So on one hand I can be impressed with this man's stewardship of his property, but on the other hand, whenever I drive by his bushes and trees, and the man hawk-eyes you as you drive by his property, I feel sorry for those trees. The trees just want to *be*, they just want to grow and flourish, and branch out and reproduce and reach out for the sunlight. They just want to be themselves. But instead they are perpetually pruned, trimmed, and filed to perfection.[4]

Jesus' Sermon on the Mount is an invitation to break free of the pruning and trimming that others place upon us; and also to be mindful of the ways in which we spend our money, speak our language, and treat others, so that we do not trim and prune others into oppression. Clearly, following Jesus no longer alleviates us of our mourning, or our poverty, but Jesus opens the doorway that leads us out of the darkness of our own prisons and into the light that leads out of the tunnels in which we often find ourselves. And now the impetus is upon ourselves to decide whether we accept this blessing selfishly or enact it as a way of finding our own salvation and inviting the Good News to be heard among those who are far less fortunate than ourselves.

You are the Salt of the Road!

Genesis 19:15-26, Matthew 5:13-16 (Epiphany 5)

This week we hear the second part of Jesus' famous sermon on the mount, where Jesus claims that those who are listening to him—the poor and the oppressed—are the salt of the earth and the light of the world. We have probably heard this before, and we know that the metaphor most often is drawn to that of food, that food tastes a lot better when it's salty. And when food needs a little salt, and you have none, the food suffers. The poor will know that they have finally tasted justice in the Kingdom of Heaven by the saltiness of its flavor.

As someone who has been recently diagnosed with hypertension, I want to avoid food references to salt for now, but instead I want to consider this analogy which Jesus makes—that "you are the salt of the earth"—to *architecture*. As some of you might know, there are five kinds of columns in classical architecture: the Tuscan, the Doric, the Ionic, the Corinthian, and the Composite. The Tuscan order of architecture, from where we get the Tuscan column, is simple, strong, and does not have any ornamentation. It does its job.

The Doric order of architecture, as symbolized by the Doric column, is based on proportions—balanced, well-structured, and relying well on its design. The Ionic column is strong and beautiful at the same time, combining the strength of the Doric-style column with the Corinthian. Some believe that these were the type of columns that were built around King Solomon's temple. The Ionic column is constructed by someone with a lot of skill and a lot of time to make it correctly.

The Corinthian order of architecture is slimmer than the Ionic column but it is more beautiful than the Ionic. The most important aspect of the Corinthian column is its engravings, and it serves to inspire the imagination as much as it is to hold up a building. The Composite order of architecture is an offshoot of the Corinthian style, but it is fancier and emphasizes more curves in its ornamentation. For this reason, it is considered to be more feminine and was very popular for the construction of churches during the Renaissance.

When we think about these five pillars we can see that they are all a little different and they build off of each other. They are often more similar than different, but they come from different points in history, and different geographical places.[1]

I'd like us to consider that the roles we often take in church reflect these orders of architecture. Some of us are Tuscan, we are the industrious pillars. Those of us who are Tuscan often do a lot of the work and aren't credited with much; it's often a thankless enterprise. I think of anyone who has worked in a church cemetery in this way, because few really know what is required to keep up a cemetery. Those of us who are Ionic columns have special skills that we use to help the church. Many of you are very gifted craftsmen or work in fabric arts and your talents are literally all around us in this church. Sometimes we take for granted how much work and skill goes into your contributions but we notice them often.

Those of us who are Corinthian pillars have good imaginations and good visions for the future, and the church as a whole at this time in history is in desperate need of men and women who are willing to do the hard work of visioning and *dreaming dreams*.[2] And along with visioning for the future, Corinthian pillars inspire others to move towards that vision.

And finally, the Composites are the show-offs, but show-offs in a good way; the Composites do acts of justice, acts of charity, and good things in our community as a result of the spiritual food they have received from their faith. Composites inspire others to go and do good things outside of the church. Often Composites are the women and grandmothers—the true pillars of the church—who work hard and pray hard to raise their children to be moral adults. Sometimes the work of Composites is noticed and celebrated and very often the hard work of Composites goes unnoticed but the visible results are often in plain view.

Many of us can perhaps see ourselves in one of the five styles of column or orders of architecture. But *then* I think about the story of the destruction of Sodom and Gomorrah, and the pillar of salt that remained of Lot's wife, for no other reason than looking back on the destruction that lies behind her, even after God told her not to look back.

For so many of us, we aspire to be like the columns of the great orders of architecture—the Tuscan, the Doric, the Ionic, the Corinthian, and the Composite, all strong and inspiring with different gifts—and at different points in our lives, when we are at our best, we are pillars of our communities, or our families and circles of friends, or the church, or even better yet, we are pillars of the mystical Body of Christ. But so often, the baggage that hangs around our necks, or the weight of the past weighs us down like an anvil on our backs and prevents us from moving on in our lives and being the strong pillars that we are often called to be; instead we are constantly looking back at our past and events from the past and feel that we cannot escape them. And not only can we often not escape the past but we are burdened by it, and what's worse, *we are sometimes punished by it.* Often we are not pillars of our community, but instead we are little more than pillars of salt.

The Good News is that Jesus speaks to all of us who are *salty pillars.* Jesus knows that history is written on the backs of those who suffer and those who sacrifice the most, and those people are Jesus' people. When Jesus says to his audience of the down-and-out, the downtrodden, and the unemployed and the oppressed that "you are the salt of the earth," Jesus is not just saying that *you* are essential to the world, or that you are what makes the world a better place. Here Jesus is speaking not so much about your value as a commodity, but that *God understands what it means to be salty*, what it means to be a pillar of salt in our world, run-down and down-and-out. The world might shame you, and history might even tell false stories about you when you're gone, and others may lie and back-stab you, but *God is with us in our saltiness*, because God is shamed, and lied about, and eulogized falsely, and used for false witness for the wicked.

So to walk the Christian walk is to live in this tension between *being a pillar* of the Body of Christ, strong and bold, with spiritual fruit and gifts, and *being a pillar of salt*, honest, meek, and bogged down by the past. It is within this ambiguous gray area where we meet Jesus, for if we were strong pillars all of the time, we would learn to be too bold and too strong and thus misunderstand our boldness as a special kind of blessing over and against those who are down-and-out. And if we were just pillars of salt all of the time we would wallow in our shame and guilt, and never come out into the light, where God calls us to be. And we would just die of saltiness, or hypertension and high blood pressure.

We can only walk this path of tension, between strength and saltiness, with the help and witness of others, helping others when they need it and seeking help when we need it, building together the Body or Temple of Christ in the present. This is what I believe Jesus meant when he said that the Kingdom of God is near and at hand. I believe Jesus meant this when he said it: *the Kingdom of God is in our hands*, when we join them together as a church and extend the hand of friendship, love, and charity.

Between Necrophilia and Biophilia!

Deuteronomy 30:15-20 (Proper 1)

In our reading from the book of Deuteronomy, Moses is given promises from God. The bottom line of these promises is that if the faithful nation stays in the ways of God, and follows his commandments, they will always live and they will prosper. If "you turn away from God," the scripture says, "you will perish," but if you "choose life," you and your children will prosper.

We all know that this isn't how we really experience the world. Very often we do everything right and everything goes wrong. This is true on the job market right now, for those of you looking for work, that even being qualified for a job *disqualifies* you for a job, because sometimes an unwritten job requirement is that an employer wants someone unqualified so that he or she can be trained the way the employer wants to justify the under-payment of the new hire. We all know today that many of our best and brightest young people go to college and graduate school and some even earn doctorates, and even then our best and brightest are unable to secure meaningful employment. My point isn't so much about higher education, but about doing everything right—you could be doing everything that would have guaranteed you a job 10 years ago, and now doing exactly those things might disqualify you completely from working at all.

Doing everything right is not always a promise that you get what you want. We all know this to be a fact of life, though we lie to our children about it all of the time. It stinks to be doing every-thing you should be doing for your work, for your family, for your relationships, and it just doesn't ever seem to go right.

But what I find most stunning about this passage of scripture from Deuteronomy is that God is ascribed to the idea of "life" here, that "God is life itself." We might often say that "God is life" without taking a moment to think what this might mean. Here "life" itself is seen to be the ultimate good, as opposed to death. But then how do we make sense of those who get sick and die? Is sickness and death a way that God is punishing them, or punishing someone else? Regardless the message given to us is that if we are to choose, if we are choosing life we are choosing God. *Choosing anything but God is to choose death.*

*

As I was thinking about preaching this message over this past week I kept thinking of the tension that we find even within our sanctuary that states something quite differently, namely, *the cross of Christ.* Saint Paul states that we are to preach Christ crucified, that is, we are to preach the death of Christ. For me it is enormously important for Christianity to understand that Christ, as God, dies on the cross, and even while he lives again on Easter Sunday, death is essential and necessary to his risen body.

When we consider the history of Christianity we think that Jesus died, rose, and ascended into heaven, the church started and shortly thereafter Europe became Christian. This is just not true. As most of us in this congregation come from German backgrounds, we know that we Germans are a stubborn people, and the Germanic tribes in Europe were very slow to convert to Christianity and there were, and still are, tinges of this Germanic paganism latent in German culture, which Hitler was famously able to manipulate in his rise to power. But Christianity did not fully penetrate the area we now call Germany for many, many centuries, and one of the reasons for this is that German paganism venerated the symbol of the tree as the ultimate source of life—the symbol of the "tree of life." The pagan Germans could not get past the notion of having a worship space with a dead tree, as a cross, with a dead body nailed to it, as in the symbol of the crucifix which is very popular in Catholicism. The German people found this symbol absolutely offensive, that Christianity was a religion that venerated death, and not life, as the symbol of life, the tree, would be killed and then a corpse would be nailed to it.[2]

Now, if you can hold onto this idea for a moment, you may have noticed that most Protestant churches do not have a crucifix, but we have an empty cross, as we do in this sanctuary. The reason given for this is usually that Catholics place more emphasis on Good Friday, the day that Jesus died, in their religion, and that Protestants celebrate Easter more, so we have the empty cross. This is all true, but we should remember that Protestantism is a German invention, and Germans were very skeptical of the whole notion of taking the very symbol of life, killing it, and venerating a dead body on the cross as a religious symbol.

The feminist philosopher of religion, Mary Daly, who died last year, wrote that the tension between good religion and bad religion is whether it *lusts for life* or *lusts for death*. Daly wrote in her critique of Christian history that the German people generally rejected Christianity not just because they were pagans and wrapped up in those traditions, but because the symbol of the dead tree and the dead body were false symbols of a false religion—that Christianity worshipped and lusted for death, rather than lusted for life. This philosopher called the lusting for death "necrophilia" and the lusting for life "biophilia."[3]

You have probably seen religious symbols of Christ on the cross that emphasize the death or the wounding or the bleeding of Christ; if you've seen the film, *The Passion of the Christ,* you know that the torture of Jesus in the film is blatantly unrealistic, that you watch Jesus bleed to death three times before he is finally killed.[4] This is the kind of lusting for death that the Germans found suspicious and blatantly offensive about

Christianity. The problem they had with Christianity is that it is *necrophilial*, or lusting for death, and that Christianity venerates the violent death of Jesus.

Yet here in the book of Deuteronomy we have God saying to *choose life*, that *God is life*, and we are directed to live towards life, even as we have the cross where God himself chooses death over life. It seems to me that we are all inching slowly towards our own deaths, and this is unavoidable. Obviously, some of us are closer to death than others, and some of us are more prepared to die than others. Some of us may die very unexpectedly when we leave church today—so everyone wear your seat-belts. I hate to be kind of a downer so close to Valentine's Day, but we all need to understand that our deaths are inevitable. *None of us are getting out alive.*

But against this reality of death, God instructs us to *choose life* and to *live life*, and to *lust for life*, even when death occurs all around us, even when we ourselves are dying. God is life, and the God who is crucified is not a god of death, as the Germans suspected, but the Crucified Christ is a God who invites us into an opportunity to *choose life* even against the reality of death, and not simply because there is no other option. To follow Christ into death, and to be baptized into Christ's death, is to follow his life, which is a life of sacrifice, but it is also a life of resurrection and living out the love of God in ways that were unable to be comprehended before.

But so often we know that church experience and Christianity is fixated upon death, that Christianity is not so much about our life or our quality of life, but it is about getting that first-class plane ticket into the Pearly Gates. When this is the primary message of our faith, ours is a cheap Christianity that believes that the cost of discipleship has no value. So often Christians are focused upon lifestyles that are seen as leading to Hell, or decisions that lead to death, or valuing certain kinds of life over the lives of others—but the God who is *biophilic*, and calls us into a lusting for life, leads us into a religious life that seeks out life and promotes life—not life necessarily in biological terms but life that is understood by way of the cross. That is, a life that is well-lived, a life that is faithful, and a life that is fruitful in the Spirit: a life that sacrifices and is thoughtful, a mindful and examined life.

Our culture, including our religious culture, regularly teaches us to lust for death, rather than to lust for life. In fact, our ways of being and behavior often teach us to do self-destructive things rather than seek out the new life that is available to us in Christ. So when we look at the cross, and when we say we carry our own cross as Christians, the question we have to answer is whether this cross is a symbol of life, or a symbol of death? Or can we conceive of a Christian way that leads the cross to be the intersection of our lusting for life with the inevitability of our own finitude and death?

The Good Catastrophe

Matthew 6:24-34 (Epiphany 8)

We Americans always want *more.* Have you ever considered that part of our identity as citizens of the United States is that we love to *have things* and we *always want more.*

Many of us have recently received a check in the mail as part of our "Economic Stimulus Package" from President George W. Bush.[1] The whole idea behind these checks being cut is that many believe that it's good for the economy if we have an extra thousand dollars to spend, so we'll go to the local department store and buy that freezer we've been thinking about getting. Not too many people are asking where this money is really coming from; I assume we just printed out some money to give away, but then we, in turn, will ask why our currency has been devalued while we blindly accept free money from the government.

A church where I used to work, that has kept me on their mailing list, actually sent all church members a letter from the Senior Pastor. The letter said that since we really don't need this money from the federal government, a great idea would be to sign it over to the church for their homeless missions. I think that is not a bad idea.

We should recall that after the terrorist attacks of September 11, 2001, our President told us all to go to church that Sunday, and on national television he suggested that we all go out and buy that American car or that American-made refrigerator that we've been thinking about to stimulate the economy. *Don't hoard your money,* President Bush advised us, *spend it.* Spending is good for the economy.

Now we know that our economy is largely dependent upon what economists sometimes call the "consumer confidence index," which you might hear being discussed regularly on the news. This index measures how confident the average American is to spend more money for his or her necessities in a given time period. The reality is that we are all learning that the consumer confidence index is very much connected to how our economy works. There is only so much money to go around, and given its scarcity, we need to fight each other for the money. When the consumer confidence index goes up, that is good news for those who sell things, and means that those of us who are looser with our wallets are a little quicker to spend our money.

But some of the cultural mechanisms around us want us to be ignorant of our finances and our economy. We all know that business education has been cut from many schools; so many people my age and younger do not understand the responsibility of credit cards to the point that it's common to hear of 30-year-olds with $20,000 or more of debt *just from credit cards alone*. The tightening up of the availability of student loan funds is making it more and more necessary to put the living expenses of college, medical, and graduate students onto credit cards just to graduate from school. If you don't believe me, tune into *The Suze Orman Show* on cable and listen to the young people who call in to her show for advice. Some have alleged that one reason why business education has been intentionally cut from public school curricula is because, again, *it's good for business—and it's good for America— when we spend too much*. The problem that we have facing us now is that too many people are spending too much and the entire economic situation feels as if it is going to have a *catastrophic collapse*.

We even think about the apocalypse of what could happen when we talk about our gas prices on the rise. I was happy to only be paying $3.55 per gallon of gas there, since gas is always more expensive in Pennsylvania. After appearing before Congress to explain themselves last week, the oil industry's executives took out full-page ads in major newspapers to defend their *apparently exploited* position: they have to raise prices on everyone when the cost of oil goes up and the value of the dollar goes down.

Money is one of the biggest things we worry about and it seems that it's on our minds lately even more than it was before. Money is the largest cause of divorce in our country. Money is almost always the cause of friendships and families to break apart. Money is a significant cause of suicide. Money is almost always the reason why churches succeed or churches fail. I once counseled a woman who had turned to prostitution because her older brother got into a tremendous amount of gambling debt and kept digging him and his family into a giant hole, quite literally. If you spend any time talking to convicts who are in prison for any amount of time, gambling and gambling addictions are almost always part of the mix of stories. Yet here in Pennsylvania, despite knowing all of this, we have invited the casinos into the state with open arms and a big welcome mat.

Our Gospel message this morning addresses the very *center* of the Gospel's message for how we are to live our day-to-day lives and how we are to think about our finances. And I think if we can remember the titles of three popular songs, we can remember the main points.

First, you may know the song "Gotta Serve Somebody" by Bob Dylan, and it's actually based on the first part of today's scripture reading. If you know the song, Dylan sings over and over again that it doesn't matter who you are, and it doesn't matter what you do, you are serving somebody. The chorus sings, "It may be the Devil, and it may be the Lord, but you're gonna have to serve somebody."[2]

Jesus teaches us, "no one can serve two masters" and "you cannot serve God and wealth." This is not a partial teaching, it is an absolute statement: *You cannot serve God and wealth.* It's true that we all have to make a living somehow, but we shouldn't get wrapped up in the work or in the money that we make. We also know people (often pastors, right?) who are married to their work in unhealthy ways, and many of *us* are gathered here in worship this morning. We also know people who may hate or love their jobs but *money motivates every aspect of their lives.* The words of Jesus cannot really be twisted around, no matter how hard we might try with interpretive or hermeneutic games: *No one can serve two masters. You cannot serve God and wealth.*

Ultimately, how we serve our Master is a choice. I don't think that Jesus' message for us today is to quit our jobs. Rather, the message is to begin or continue the *cataclysmic,* if not *apocalyptic, shift in our life focus away from money, and power, and drugs, and drink or whatever else we worship instead of God alone* toward *God alone,* and not simply just anything we name "God" but a *God that cannot be objectified or idolatrized.* If we make this God beyond anything idolatrized as "God" at the center of our lives, we begin to *think and do God* in every aspect of our lives. To live this way is to *live an ecology of God,* to *live in* and *live with* God constantly.[3] We might come to church on Sundays, but when we live this way the real worship occurs in our mundane, everyday lives and banal decision-making. This is to live our lives with real *reverence:* constantly offering our lives for the divine in worship, and especially outside of these church doors, Monday through Saturday. When we live this way we are radically changing and *reversing* by transforming our lives and transforming the ecologies in which we inhabit beyond the walls of this sanctuary.

Just as Bob Dylan sang in his song, "You're gonna have to serve somebody," we too need to ask, who are we serving? Who is really our Master? A good indication of who we are *really* serving might stem from the *second* song title that I want you to remember: "Don't Worry, Be Happy."[4]

Don't worry, be happy. This is one of those few songs just about everyone across the generations knows. This song does not come from the Bible, but its message is our Biblical message for today.

Jesus teaches: Just look at the birds. They don't seem to worry, and somehow they persevere. It is obvious that God takes care of the birds. Jesus also asks: Look at all of the flowers, does not God make them beautiful in their season?

Here is Jesus' answer, taken right from the Bible: "Therefore, do not worry, saying, what will we eat? Or what will we drink? Or what will we wear?" He continues, saying, those who do not trust in God are obsessed with these things, and God knows that we need to eat, and we need to drink, and we need to be clothed. *Obviously*, if there is a God in heaven, such a God would know these facts. So, we should not be *obsessed* with these things. We should *not worry*, but simply, *be happy. Don't worry, be happy.*

I love the way that the Bible paraphrase, *The Message*, translates these words: "Look at the birds, free and unfettered, not tied down to a job description, careless in the care of God. And you [as in each and every one of us] count far more to him than birds." Jesus continues: "If God gives such attention to … wildflowers [and birds]—most of which are never seen—don't you think he'll attend to you, take pride in you, do his best for you? What I'm trying to do here is get you to relax, to not be so preoccupied with *getting* so you can respond to God's *giving*. People who don't know God and the way he works fuss over these things, but you know both God and how he works." Then Jesus says: "Steep your life in God-reality, God-initiative, God-provisions. Don't worry about missing out. You'll find all your everyday human concerns will be met."

Is this not the *heart* of what the Gospel is for us? Is this not what we need to teach our children so that they are not plagued with the disease of which we are all contagious?—This *disease of consumerism* that seeps out of nearly every aspect of our lives? Don't we need to teach this openly to all of our teenagers? Don't we know someone close to us who needs to hear these words *every single day*? Is this not the message we all need to affirm *every moment of every day:* "Steep your life in *God-reality, God-initiative, God provisions?*" The Good News is good indeed, namely, that God *includes* all of us, but we must *exclude* all that is not Godly from our lives. Following Jesus to—and I *love* how Jesus puts this—*live in God-reality* leads us to sometimes *exclude* things from our lives. (And clearly, I'm *not* talking about the *exclusion of people*, which is what we in the church so often do rather than face our own demons.)

Sometimes following God leads us to be left out of the crowd. For me, I have had to walk away from churches and denominational systems that I found to be hurtful, evil, and contrary to the message of radical inclusion which Jesus demands. It is painful and hurtful to be exclusionary, to walk away from the Gospel of false exclusivity, to *exclude* Satanic *exclusivism*. We must walk these trails with the confidence to wear God on our sleeves, and doing so will always lead some "Christians" to simply exclude us. We should recall that the philosopher Søren Kierkegaard taught that Christians should always do the very opposite of what "the crowd" wants and does, because "the crowd" wants easy answers, and *Christianity is* (contrary to popular practice) *the religion of no easy answers*. Rather, God is all that ultimately matters, and the love of God is all we need, and it is often very difficult in practice to fully accept the Gospel of God's love in our whole lives.

Jesus in on to something in our culture here. We all need to *not worry, and be happy*—not for the sake of just being happy, but *happy in the faith* that we are valued and loved. Happy in the belief that living with God leads us to happiness. And in this *happiness*, we *don't need to worry*. We just need to *be happy*.

To review: The first song title to remember is "You're Gonna Have to Serve Somebody," the second was "Don't Worry, Be Happy." Our third song title to remember is the hymn, "Seek Ye First." You know this hymn: "Seek ye first the kingdom of God," right out of our scripture reading for today.[5]

Jesus teaches that in being left out of the crowd, we are *excluded* from the world that strives for that which is ungodly, and we are to "seek first for the kingdom of God and his righteousness," as the song goes. For "God will give you the kingdom of God," assuring us not to "worry about tomorrow." We don't have to worry about tomorrow? We don't have to worry about tomorrow! This *'don't worry, be happy'* bit sounds pretty great! *Not so fast,* for there's more. When Jesus finishes his sermon he warns us about tomorrow: "tomorrow will bring about worries of its own. Today's trouble is enough for today." *Oh.* That doesn't sound as carefree as it would have, had I only read half of the message.

The Catholic author and scholar J.R.R. Tolkien, famous for his *Lord of the Rings* books, wrote that the Christian message is a "eucatastrophe."[6] A eucatastrophe is a *good catastrophe.* What would it mean to say that the Christian message is a *good catastrophe?*

Have you ever met someone who is really annoying?—That's a ridiculous question! I don't mean annoying in the sense that the person does things that are annoying, but someone *whose entire being* is *absolutely annoying?* I used to work with someone who was so happy all of the time that I just could not stand it when I first met her. Everything was happy around her. In fact, one day I thought I saw the raindrops bend around her when it was raining; she didn't get wet. She spoke in a voice like an operatic *recitative,* quite literally *singing,* all of the time. Including staff meetings; *I could not stand how damn happy she was all of the time.*

One time during a staff meeting, this happy woman's pen ran out of ink. She used the happiest pens ever, they were pink with pink puffy things all over them. She actually got pretty aggravated that this pen that looked as if it had taken the down from some endangered bird *ran out of ink!* She was flustered and confused! *And I enjoyed watching her.*

But then she pulled out of her purse this very thick, electric pink pen with these huge peacock-looking feathers on the pen! And she smiled, and interrupted whoever was speaking at the meeting, singing, "*Thank God that old pen went dry, because I have been just dying* to get this new pen out to write with." She giggled and shivered with happiness, and we all looked at each other in the meeting and went on with business.

I know that *you all know* someone just like this.

I learned, however, while getting to know this colleague better over the years that this woman was no phony. I learned to appreciate how her happiness was magnetic towards other people. I also learned that she had a number of close friends who died fairly young. Her parents also died fairly young as well. When the tech stocks tumbled a few years ago, her family lost nearly everything. Beyond all of these things, she had successfully fought off cancer not once, *but twice*. She was lucky — *very lucky* — to be alive.

For many people, all of the bad things that have happened to this woman would have been reason enough to declare defeat on life or at least give up on their faith. Yet she is the happiest person I have ever met. *This* kind of happiness, I believe, is a genuine *Christian happiness* that arises from the darkness of defeat. It is a happiness that has carried the crucifixion through the tough times: a happiness born out of the death of God on the cross. I honestly don't think this woman would have been so happy had all of those bad things not have happened to her. As the philosopher Friedrich Nietzsche said, and many of you have surely heard this statement, "What does not kill me makes me stronger."

This *eucatastrophe*, this *good catastrophe* is the Kingdom of Christ embodied. This *good catastrophe* is what Jesus calls us to *seek first*. This Kingdom is *not* a saccharine-coated Gospel. It is not a Gospel of Wealth or a Gospel of Absolute Inclusion that we can do and participate in and afford to buy all things. *Quite the opposite:* the eucatastrophic Gospel calls us to be exclusive in our wants, so that we might focus our lives upon taking on this world in a Christ-like manner.

Jesus might have started his career, as the Gospel of Matthew indicates, in the northern lakeside villages of Capernaum, which had spas where the wealthy hung out, but Jesus quickly descended himself and humbled himself in his ministries to the sick, and to the poor and to the outcasts—to the prostitutes and to the lepers. As such the Kingdom of God is not in the temples but decidedly *outside of the temples*, and is located not in the center of civil or genteel society but rather *on the margins of society.* The Kingdom of God is taking up the cross upon which God himself died, and descending into Hell. *Happily descending into Hell, living the death of God through the pain, through this catastrophe of life, through the tragedy that is on the periphery of the world—often hidden from us.* Jesus instructs: "Seek *this* first."

One of the lessons of our Christian calendar is that we can only arrive at Easter by way of Good Friday and by way of Holy Saturday: we cannot skip the death of God on the cross, we cannot skip the descent into Hell. We Protestants try hard to avoid these theological concepts even while we celebrate their holidays. But we must never forget the final triumph that is the resurrection, even if it is only through the good catastrophe that is life lived genuinely, so that we may one day arrive at a complete and ultimate joy.

God's Tattoos

Isaiah 49:8-16a (Proper 3)

Lady GaGa's massive pop song hit, "Born This Way" was released in early February, 2010, and was creating a little bit of a buzz among progressive Christian circles because of the explicitly liberal Christian message preached in the song. The sermon isn't about the song but picks up on its themes.

Our reading this morning is from the book of Isaiah, written during the time of the Babylonian Exile, when the Jews were taken into slavery out of their country by oppressors who tried to destroy their civilization, their religion, and their culture. The message is that despite all hardship, despite the odds, despite everything working against God's people, and even despite the faithlessness of God's people, God still loves them. And the love of God is not just freely given as a gift but it is part of God's own identity.

The last lines of the poem of our Isaiah reading are a response to the prayer many of us might often have offered, "Why, God, have you forgotten me?" Why do all of the bad things in the world need to happen to me? God replies: "Can a woman forget her nursing child? Can a woman show no compassion for the child of her womb?"

The answer to this question is almost rhetorical in our current situation where it is very easy for a woman to get an abortion—and we probably all know someone who has made the decision to abort a child and the morality of abortion is not our conversation for today. But when God compares Godself to a pregnant woman, we can say that we could conceive of someone not loving the child in her womb. But we can move away from this simplistic way of thinking about this image into the question of what this metaphor means, rather than what the words indicate on a literal level. In other words, to the question, "Can a woman forget her nursing child or show no compassion to the child of her womb?" we can answer, yes, actually, we can believe such a situation. But we are talking about God, so we are talking about an ideal of faithfulness. We can consider that God is not faithful to us, but we know that God would not be God if we were to think in these terms.

The next words of God's reply to the question, "God, why have you forgotten me?" are "Even these may forget"—in other words, even *those* who I always bless and even those who always get the job or are always on top may forget God—but, God says, "yet I will not forget you." No matter how bad we might mess up, God loves us as a child God has carried in her womb in expectation that we will eventually come around and be good children that will make a proud parent. This is to say, some only thank God when they win the Super Bowl or win the award, but you, as my good child, God says, thank me when the going is tough and when you're on the down-and-out.

The final line of our reading is a simple statement; God says, "See, I have inscribed you on the palms of my hands." This isn't saying that God is inscribed on *our* hands, but *we are inscribed* on God's hands. Our faithfulness *changes* God and is part of God's plan for all of history.

We should remember that palm reading has been around for thousands of years, and we know that an instruction manual on palm reading was written in India about the same time as this poem was written, during the Babylonian exile. We should assume that the reference here is to palm reading. In palmistry, as it is called, it is believed that one can predict future events based on the markings of your hands; palm readers call this technique "chiromancy," using the lines to indicate life events, premature death, marriage, children, and so on. The ancient Greeks, with whom the Jews writing down the book of Isaiah would have been familiar, practiced this kind of palm reading by associating different areas of your dominant hand, the hand you write with, to different Gods and their characteristics. The design on your palms in the different god-zones on your hands indicated the attributes that these Gods gave you before you were born. And reading your palms was a way of discovering the Gods' plans for you and your life.

Here in the Bible we have something quite different indeed, namely, a *reversal* of palmistry.

God proclaims, through the prophet, that God does not mark *our* hands in terms of his grand design for the universe, but instead *we are the markings of God's hands*. In these simple words — "See, I have inscribed you in the palms of my hands" — we actually find a very direct *reversal* of what would have been some of the popular spiritual thinking of the day. Perhaps to use a modern example, it isn't us that gets the tattoo on our arm with the word "mother," but it's God who gets a tattoo to honor us, before we're born. In other words, we're a permanent part of God's identity, even while we can deny God in any number of ways throughout our own lives.

To say that we are marked upon the body of God is to say that God has an ultimate role for us, but this role isn't really about us, *it's about God*, and it's about our lives being the hands of God, for God in the world. There is no temporal future to predict other than to draw close to the God who nurtures us and calls us home. The absolute urgency is on us in the present to build the Kingdom of God in our own ways, using the gifts God has for us, even when times are tough.

The Good News is that we are not only called to do this simply because we are to be obedient to God, or that we *owe* it to God, but because we have a loving relationship with God, like a mother that lovingly knitted us together in her womb and a mother who smiles with pride in her children who love her unconditionally as a reflection of her unconditional love. And we know that our mothers carry the battle scars for their children, often throughout their lives.

We can deny God through the worship of our wealth and privilege, the worship of other gods, the worship of our relationships, and the worship of ourselves. But we cannot deny that we were not just born with God's fingerprints upon us, but more radically, our mark is on God so deeply and so obviously that God not only cannot deny us, but God would not deny us. And furthermore, God's plan for the universe requires us to be God's hands and face for others to "come home to mamma."

Preparing Again for the Death of God

Matthew 17:1-9 (Transfiguration Sunday)

Many Christians believe that one of the biggest challenges of our modern era for the church is the challenge of contemporary atheism against Christian belief. I have always been fascinated by the question of atheism and the arguments for and against the existence of God; in fact in graduate school I took an entire semester-long course on one of the more famous arguments for the existence of God called "the ontological argument" of Saint Anselm, studying this argument for the existence of God from every possible direction imaginable.

But what has always piqued my interest was the death of God theology that emerged in the 1960s. Some of you might remember the Easter issue of *Time* magazine, April 6, 1966, with the words, "Is God Dead?"[1] Many churches and pastors did not read the article that was the cover story of this magazine, which then became the best-selling issue of *Time* in its history, but many Christians were simply offended that theology professors at religious universities, including one who was an ordained minister (Paul M. van Buren), had declared God is dead.

What these theologians were saying was that, at bottom, our understanding of God must change. The 1960s was a time of revolution in every part of our culture, from politics to music; with all of these radical revolutions, the death of God theology was the call to the church to change. The refusal of the church to change led to a new generation of church-based nostalgia and a younger generation of people looking to eastern religions and new religious movements, and many more to reject the idea of religion altogether as a cultural force that apprehends change and revolution. As the Bob Dylan song went, "The Times, they are a-changin,"[2] and a generation—in fact the generation that many of you are part of—generally rejected the church and never really looked back.

The death of God theology, however, beyond what the magazine reported, really taught that as our old conceptions of God must die: the idea of a bearded man in the sky who dictates his will to lemming-servants within the church, or the idea of God mandating war or colonial power to nations of people of color throughout the world. *These images of God must die*; so also must we understand that not only must our images of God change with the times, but we must also understand that *God changes with us.*

The religious literalist will often retort, "but it says in the Bible that God never changes!" We should recall that the *whole point of Christianity* is that *God changes*, and not just a little change, but *God enacts a radical change upon Godself*, incarnating into a person on earth. That person preached *change* and of a tremendous *reversal* that must occur that he called the Kingdom of God. We are called to respond to that *change* by enacting and embodying *change*. Christianity is undeniably a *religion of change*. That said, in today's Bible reading we find Jesus *changing*, undergoing a metamorphosis, in preparation for the last month of his life. This event is called the transfiguration, where Jesus exhibits an outward change to those around him. Our liturgical calendar celebrates Transfiguration Sunday before the beginning of the season of Lent every year.

The notion that God is changing, or that God is *change-itself*, is still a controversial issue within Christianity, mostly because we like images of God with which we are comfortable and accustomed. We like the safety of God lying in repose. Consequently, this is what the death of God theology taught, but more importantly this is also what the New Testament teaches, namely, *that our old conceptions of God must change when we change ourselves with and through Christ*. And since Christianity is in the business of change, we should promote change.

If you think about this a little with me, when we say that we become a Christian, this indicates a change in our lives, or at least it should. When we are baptized or confirmed, it indicates a change or transition. When we get married, the ritual itself and its blessing by the community is a formal change of our lives. And we are constantly changing throughout our lives.

But so often Christians believe that they are at some point "born again" and they don't have to keep changing. What the transfiguration of Jesus suggests is that God can undergo a radical change by coming into the world as a baby at Christmas, and change again with the transfiguration, and then continue to change on through the death of God on the cross on Good Friday and the return of Jesus on Easter Sunday.

And then after Easter, God *keeps changing* by revealing himself as the resurrected Christ and then ascending to heaven, and God then changes again when the Holy Spirit comes down from the sky on the Day of Pentecost.

Now, I just gave you the quick tour of a Confirmation class of the church calendar of Christmas-Epiphany-Transfiguration-Lent-Good Friday-Easter-Ascension-and-Pentecost. But the Good News is that at Pentecost God enacts his changing self upon us, and now we are to enact the change of God for ourselves and for the world.

Just as the old manifestation of God dies, another one is born at every new moment of the Christ story, and we live the death and resurrection of God when our lives reflect the movement of God that we can know as revealed from the scriptures. This is one of the deepest meanings of our baptism and it is, quite directly, the meaning of being a "Christian" as a follower of Christ, as one who follows Christ through the changes of life, and into a life of bearing one's own cross for the sake of others.

This might sound very abstract but the point of this is that being a Christian is not simply living a changed life, but living a *changing* life. When someone says that one has to be born again to be a Christian, we know that to believe in a God that has not only transfigured but is transfiguring is to be born again and to die again, to live out the promises of our baptism every day that we are blessed to be awakened in the morning.

On the other hand, to simply believe that we are born again and then, because we have been born again, we must work to keep ourselves, the church, and the culture to be the same and as similar to that moment of our own born again experiences as possible *is to deny the true changing power of God in the world and to perpetuate a belief in a God that is a distant memory of the past.* In other words, *to cling to the religion of the past is a deep kind of atheism that apprehends a God who is still speaking in the present, speaking to us and through us.*

To return to the challenge of atheism in our contemporary world, I do not believe that philosophical or scientific atheism is the true threat to authentic Christian thinking in the world, but rather, it is *the atheism that the church itself breeds* for which we must be most mindful.[3] This atheism *denies* the ever-present changing power of God in the present, this atheism *relegates* the greatest deeds of God to be in dusty stories of the past, and this atheism *seeks to hold the church back*—holding the church *in exile*— from engaging the world and our culture in new and relevant ways. One might even say that the general state of the church today is that it is full of atheists, in this sense of the term, as an institution stuck in the past.

I believe that there are people outside of the church searching, yearning, hungry, and *thirsting* for a forward-looking faith, and I believe that there are many of these seekers in our community. The impetus is now upon all of us to represent this transfiguration to our neighbors, friends, and families, and to continue this transfiguration throughout our lives in every aspect of our living.

The Season of Lent

Re-membering the Dis-membered

Genesis 2:15-17, 3:1-7; Matthew 4:1-11 (Lent 1)

Shortly after being baptized, Jesus goes into the wilderness for forty days and forty nights, fasting, and at the end of his fasting, the devil appears to him. The devil tempts Jesus into making a magic trick, of transfiguring or changing stones to become loaves of bread. But Jesus says no.

Then the devil took Jesus to the highest point of the temple, and said, if you are God, allow yourself to fall to safety. And Jesus says no. And then the devil brought Jesus to a high mountain, and there Jesus is offered all of the kingdoms of the world, if he would worship the devil. And Jesus says no again.

What I find so interesting about this is that the devil is actually tempting Jesus to do the things which Jesus himself later accomplishes. The devil tempts Jesus to transfigure an object into something else. Not only does Jesus transfigure himself, as we discussed last week, but he later turns water into wine, turns dead people into living people, and later institutes the changing of bread and wine into his body and blood. So Jesus says no to the devil, but he in fact does enact transfiguration later in the story.

And the devil tempts Jesus to cheat death from the highest point of the temple. Now it would have been considered blasphemous for anyone to comprehend that they could stand atop the holy temple in Jerusalem and command the angels to carry him down, yet Jesus elsewhere blasphemes directly against the temple, and as the story goes, Jesus conquers death in the act of the resurrection. Jesus is then carried away by angels on the Day of Ascension, escaping the coming destruction of the Temple, having been transfigured and ready to enter the spiritual temple of the angels. So Jesus again says no to the devil, but later he goes on to defy human death.

The devil then offers Jesus lordship of all that is on earth, to be above every living king and to be the god above all other gods in the world. Jesus says no again, saying famously, "Away with you, Satan, for it is written, 'Worship the Lord your God, and serve only him.'"

Again, what the devil is offering to Jesus is in fact what we believe about Jesus, and what we sing about Jesus nearly every Sunday. I immediately think of the prayer hymn, "He is Lord": "Every knee shall bow, and every tongue confess that Jesus Christ is Lord."[1] And also the Hallelujah chorus from Handel's *Messiah*: "King of Kings ... and Lord of Lords." So what I am saying is that the devil offers Jesus the opportunity to become the incarnate Lord of the world, and Jesus says no thanks, because to do so would be idolatry, and he would not worship the devil to do so.

To read the scripture this way suggests to me that at the very beginning of Jesus' ministry, Jesus has the opportunity to forgo the ritual dance that will be his ministry to the poor and his eventual sacrifice that will demonstrate to everyone that he is in fact the Lord. Jesus could simply go the easy route, and skip Lent altogether, and go right to Christ the King Sunday. There would be no need for the church, apart from worshiping him; there would be no need for him to die and be raised from the dead, and there would be no need to go to Hell. There would be no need to ascend to heaven. We could make everything a whole lot easier and go straight to the Reign of Christ on earth now.

Or could it be that it is the devil giving Jesus clues for what he must eventually accomplish later as he progresses toward his execution? Is it possible that, just as the talking serpent in the book of Genesis is craftier than we thought; that the snake is working in cahoots with God to begin what must happen for history to commence from the Garden of Eden? To suggest that the evil forces or the devil works with the side of God isn't a terrible stretch; if you read the book of Genesis closely, it seems as if the snake and God were setting the first humans up.[2] And if you read the book of Job, clearly Satan is working with God.[3]

To read the Jesus story this way, Jesus meets the devil at the beginning of his ministry, and Jesus resists the devil, though it may seem as though the devil put some ideas into Jesus' head that were part of God's grandiose plan from the beginning. Jesus does not bite from the forbidden fruit, but he goes into the last chapter of his life with some new and bold ideas. Again: all of what the devil tempts happens later, except Jesus does not fall on his knees to the devil; instead Jesus is bookmarked with Jesus himself overtaking the devil once and for all on Holy Saturday.

What Jesus could have avoided—the last chapter of his life, and his death—is what we now remember as we enter into this season of Lent. Today we celebrate the sacrament of Communion as a way of remembering Jesus. Jesus chooses to remain with humanity and not enter the rank of the gods, and he chooses to remain with the poor and oppressed. Jesus here is a divided individual—man and God—but neither yet fully man nor fully God. *He is divided*, as we often are in our lives and decisions, and Jesus chooses the more difficult road to avoid worshiping the devil. The devil offers Jesus the *illusion* of wholeness: not true wholeness.

Jesus chooses to search for wholeness and purpose by not placing magic, or great spectacles, or cheating death, or political domination over the world as the beginning of his introduction to his people, but to instead live and suffer with his people, and die the death of a criminal. Jesus spiritually and physically dismembers himself so that we not only worship him because of a good deal made with the devil, but instead because he remembers us even as we too are tempted to be made whole by offers given to us by the world and not from God. Jesus *re-members* us as *dis-membered* members of his body, broken and shed for us and for many.

And in this re-membering, par-taking, and in be-coming, we

too be-come the dis-membered body of Christ, as our liturgy says, given for this harsh world that hates peace, love, and friendship. With this spirit we now reverse the wishes of Jesus, and fulfill the temptation of the devil, by singing and proclaiming that "Jesus is Lord."

Nicodemus' Secret

John 3:1-17 (Lent 2)

This passage of scripture has two of the most famous lines from the Bible. First, "you must be born again"; and second, "for God so loved the world that he gave his only begotten son, and whosoever believes in him should not perish, but have everlasting life." These two phrases are so well known that they are part of regular conversation between Christians, as in, someone asking if they are "born again" or describing themselves as a "born again Christian," or people holding up John 3:16 signs at football games.

We all know that so often these two statements are meant to be *exclusionary*, rather than *inclusive* statements of love. When Jesus says you must be born again, we often make an assumption that Jesus is probably speaking to Nicodemus about a small group of people being saved. When Jesus says that whoever believes in him will not perish but have everlasting life, very often it is not the everlasting life that is emphasized or celebrated, but instead the focus is upon the exclusion of much of the world in this great statement. And while I want to resist the exclusive or exclusivistic nature of these statements, it's hard to ignore them.

It would be helpful for us to talk about the various sub-groups of Jews that were important during the time of Jesus: The Pharisees, the Sadducees, and the Essenes. If you know your Bible and Bible history, these terms are probably familiar to you. The Pharisees were very legalistic and political, and the Bible often characterizes them as a conservative group that sought to follow their religion to the letter of the law. The Sadducees were an opposing group to the Pharisees, and were more entrenched in the political machine of Jewish culture; the Sadducees were often the tax collectors and the political administrators on behalf of the

Jewish priests.

But then there is another group called the Essenes. The Essenes are a mysterious group, and some of the speculation is that many of the Dead Sea Scrolls, found in a cave in a place called Qumran, were writings collected by the Essene community. The Essenes, some today believe, practiced a ritual of being initiated into their group by ritually burying a person while he was still alive and then resurrecting the person in ritual. The symbolism is that the initiate dies to their previous life and is born again. Those who were full members of the group were considered the "living" and those outside of the group were considered to be "dead."

Some have speculated that John the Baptist was a member of this Essene group, who were mostly secretive. The theory is that John the Baptist began preaching and practicing a kind of "second birth" ritual through water baptism outside of the Essene Community, making public a ritual that was before only known to the Essenes in secret.[1]

There is further suggestion that Jesus was either a part of this Essene community or may have been initiated into the group and then left, and in leaving he began preaching some of the secret teachings and ideas of the Essenes to everyone, instead of just a select few. Some of the stories of Jesus are opened up in new ways if one considers this to be true—for example, the raising of Lazarus would have been symbolic of Jesus restoring life to someone who was considered spiritually dead. (Or when Jesus says his famous line, "let the dead bury their own dead,"[2] this statement is an Essene belief: those outside of the sect are dead anyway, and death is an essential part of the outsiders' culture of death.) Some of these lines of thinking are esoteric or highly speculative; but are not all Biblical hermeneutics speculative in some way?

With this in mind, we now encounter Nicodemus, who is a Pharisee and a member of the Sanhedrin, or a judge. The

Pharisees were a group who did not like the Essenes, and the Essenes did not like the Pharisees. As such, Nicodemus encounters Jesus and asks him questions, trying to trick him. The story ends not knowing whether Nicodemus immediately accepts or rejects Jesus, but Jesus takes Nicodemus seriously and gives him two of the most important of all of his teachings: given to a member of a religious and political sect that Jesus, whether he was an Essene or not, would *not* have typically entertained because the Pharisees would have been seen as the enemy.

We encounter Nicodemus later in the story on two occasions. In John 7, Nicodemus is accused by the insiders of the Pharisees of being under Jesus' influence when Nicodemus demands that Jesus be treated fairly. The Pharisees pass off Nicodemus as being too friendly to Jesus because they are both from the same area, saying, "Surely there is no prophet in Galilee."[3] Even later we again encounter Nicodemus in the Gospel of John 19, where Nicodemus comes to the dead body of Jesus, bringing burial spices, including myrrh, one of the spices brought by the three wise men, and Nicodemus then ritually prepared Jesus' corpse to prepare it for burial and then laid Jesus into the tomb.[4]

So it would seem that Jesus made a convert out of Nicodemus, who approaches Jesus in an accusatory way as a Pharisee, and hears Jesus' famous teaching, "you must be born again." Perhaps Nicodemus knew that Jesus had unknowingly initiated him into the secret teachings of the Essene community and understood what Jesus was saying perhaps more than the disciples following Jesus around. In other words, Nicodemus is portrayed by John as a Jew whom the disciples, as working-class fishermen, would have never accepted—excluded because the Pharisees (the sect to which Nicodemus affiliated) despised the mainstream Jewish working class.

Regardless, in the scriptures we find that Nicodemus understood Jesus' words and came to later prepare Jesus' body with one hundred pounds of embalming material (an inordinate amount of expensive spices) because he knew that Jesus was truly the only begotten son that is spoken of in John 3:16. In fact, Nicodemus was the first to hear and the first to believe these famous words. Nicodemus tends to the deceased body of Christ, while the other disciples are in hiding and afraid. Nicodemus somehow got the hint that Jesus did not mean that eternal life was just a metaphor or a figure of speech, but that Jesus was about to enact a raising of the dead that universally follows from the resurrection of Jesus himself from the grave.

These teachings of Jesus—that you must be born again and that God loves the world so much that he gave his son—were like a *secret message*, passed in a *secret code* by Jesus to Nicodemus, and they are handed now to us through scripture. Somehow Nicodemus made the connections that no one else really did. The question posed to us now is what we are going to do with this secret information?

Christians are often in the habit to, as I said before, focus upon the exclusionary words and tone of these teachings, believing that one must be "born again" in the exact same way that they are, baptized in a certain way, voting in a certain way: all if one is to truly be a Christian. Furthermore, under the banner of John 3:16, many Christians believe that if you do not believe in Jesus the exact same way as they do, one cannot be a legitimate Christian. Churches that nationally protest funerals and local Christians who protest high school musicals, and Christians and preachers everywhere who shun members of their own families and communities are all experiences to which we can all relate as practices of exclusion.

But we need to read the line after John 3:16, which follows like this. Verse 16 reads, "For God so loved the world that he gave his only-begotten son, that whosoever believes in him should not perish but have eternal life," and now verse 17: "Indeed, God did not send the Son into the world to condemn the world, but in order that the world might be saved through him." Those who choose not to believe are condemned already, because they have not experienced the resurrection of being born again in the first place. But Jesus' resurrection invites new believers into the resurrection, a resurrection only understood by a few before, and now accessible to all.

The bottom line for this teaching is that Nicodemus understands the resurrection as a resurrection not just for some, but for many, and among those whom Jesus came to die for is Nicodemus himself, who humbles himself and publicly speaks for, and is ridiculed for his support of Jesus. And when everyone else bails on Jesus at the end, this outsider comes to prepare the body of Christ for a resurrection that will invite new people into the secret for thousands of years to come.

So the question left for us is: *Are we ready to let the secret out?*

Bring Yer Spittoon!

Psalm 23; John 9:1-41 (Lent 3)

One of my favorite pieces of church music is Anton Bruckner's hymn (or motet) *"Os Justi Meditabitur,"* which in Latin means "The Just Mouth," which is a meditation on the righteousness of the mouth of God, out of which flow the laws of the Bible. But what impresses me the most about this story of Jesus healing the blind man is, quite literally, the mouth of Jesus. More specifically, I mean his salivary glands that make his saliva.

And it isn't the healing properties of Jesus' spit but the actual quantity of saliva it would require for Jesus to do what the Bible says he does. Have you ever considered just how much saliva it would take to make a paste that would gel enough together to hold onto someone's eyes? Any ten year old boy could tell you just how impressive this is.

One time I taught this story of Jesus to a Junior High youth group and, quite honestly, the youth just could not get past their disgust and fascination with Jesus spitting and spreading it on the eyelids of the blind man. One teen said, why did Jesus have to tell him to go take a bath after he put spit on his face? Wouldn't the blind man have been like, "You don't need to tell me twice to wash off this dirt and spit from my face!"

When the Pharisees got wind of all that had happened, that the blind man had been healed, they questioned him, and they didn't believe his story so they went to his parents, who were afraid of the Pharisees and let their son speak for himself. Were the Pharisees aware that Jesus spread his spit on his face? Were the parents aware of the spit on their son's face?

So the Pharisees went back to the formerly blind man and then we see something of a kangaroo court emerge. The blind man says that Jesus healed him. The Pharisees are trying to persecute Jesus by accusing him of blaspheming openly, but the blind man says that Jesus could not be a blasphemer because the power of God works *through* Jesus, as evidenced from his own eyes being opened. The man says, "Never since the beginning of the world has blindness been cured in such a way." The Pharisees then accuse the man himself of blaspheming because they dismiss him as someone born in sin who is now trying to teach religion—even though they are the ones who brought him to trial in the first place. The line of questioning here is not on how Jesus healed the blind man, that is, through spit and dirt, but more specifically by what authority or by what means of power the healing happened. The scriptures say that the Pharisees "drove" the blind man "out," assuming to mean "out of the temple." They kicked him out of the temple.

Jesus hears that the man had been kicked out of the temple and returns to the blind man, and the blind man confesses faith that Jesus is the Son of God. While the man worships Jesus, Jesus says, "I came into this world for judgment, so that those who do not see may see and those who do see may become blind." The Pharisees nearby overhear this and ask, "He *couldn't* possibly be speaking about *us*, could he?"

*

Traditional readings of this passage of scripture focus upon the blind man's blindness as a metaphor for being removed from the light of Christ, which is an important theme throughout John's gospel. Another message of this passage of scripture is the miracle of the act of healing here, but Jesus points to the reality that the physical healing that he performs points to a deeper issue of spiritual sickness in the culture. I am a little uncomfortable sometimes with the way in which the healing stories treat disability, but an important message of this passage of scripture emphatically states that disabilities or physical ailments don't imply the sins of one's parents and that disabilities can sometimes serve a higher purpose.

So let's get right back to the spitting. We think of spitting as something derogatory, that spitting in front of someone is offensive. But spitting was actually not seen as something offensive until very recently in history. When I was in college it was a common thing that boys would walk around with empty soda bottles to spit their tobacco juice in while we were in class; in fact, every time I see a Mountain Dew bottle I think of this. And when I was a kid I went to the Lebanon Bologna Festival, which had a tobacco spitting contest for the adults and a spitting contest for the kids, which I remember because they gave us tootsie-rolls for us to chew like tobacco. This is unthinkable today, as our perceptions of spitting tobacco have changed, even in the last 15-20 years.

It could be that the reason why we might not be able to get past the spitting part of this Jesus story is because the ancient cultures had a different understanding of spitting. In fact, our culture's understanding of spitting has changed over time, and made a big change when the discovery was made that saliva carries disease. It was not until scientists discovered that saliva carries disease that spitting became a universally disgusting act.

And there are ways that spitting is used in religious ritual. In Jewish culture, during the traditional *Aleinu leshabei'ach* prayer that is often said three times per day, most Jews bow as a way of humbling themselves before God, but in some Hasidic Jewish groups the Jews actually spit on the ground as a way of humbling themselves and other idols that sometimes take the place of God. And this, we should remember, is the first Commandment, "you shall not have any other Gods before me," which is meditated upon as part of the *Aleinu* prayer.

In far Middle Eastern culture, and this practice continues in the present, mothers will sometimes spit onto the ground to the side of their children as a ritual act that symbolizes that they do not place their children above their religious obligations to God, because children very often become idols for many parents (we all know a few "helicopter parents," right?). But this act of spitting to the side of a child is not meant to be an offense to the child but a way of honoring the child and the child's relationship to God. This ritual act is also meant to be a way of protecting the mother and children from the "evil eye," or the superstitious belief that bad luck or curses may come their way from evil people looking at them.

Let's consider for a moment that Jesus' act of spitting here is ritually protecting the blind man from getting the "evil eye." The Pharisees bring the formerly blind man into the temple to *see* for themselves that he has been given *sight*. They then go to *see* Jesus for themselves. They go back to the formerly blind man, and the blind man is thrown out from their *sight*, and being thrown out of the temple is a way of saying that your life no longer has any significance within the *sight* of God.

But then Jesus returns to him, after being kicked out of the temple, and has a conversation with him, and the man says that I was once *blind* but now I *see*. Here's my point: Jesus could not have given the blind man the "evil eye," a curse with his eyes, because the blind man could not *see* Jesus before. Jesus spitting on the ground was a way by which Jesus ritually protected the blind man from the evil gaze of the Pharisees, and Jesus even sent him to the bathing pool to the south of the temple so that the Pharisees would *see* the man cured of his blindness. Twice the Pharisees encounter the man and he is not persuaded to renounce Jesus because he simply tells the truth to their questions. When the Pharisees' powers of persuasion are ineffective over the blind man, he returns to Jesus and arrives to believe in Jesus by his own reason.

So the miracle of the story is not so much that Jesus *healed* the blind man but that because *Jesus ritually offered him protection against the evil of others*, the blind man finds the freedom to accept and worship Jesus as the Son of God. While the Pharisees kicked the formerly blind man out of the temple, formally kicking an outsider out, who was already far outside of the temple in the first place, we should remember that his own parents also hung him out to dry, as well, because they were afraid that they would be cast out further from the center of the religious mainstream than they already were. By kicking the formerly blind man out, the Pharisees were attempting to protect themselves and others from the physical and spiritual impurities that this formerly blind man represented.

But Jesus' ritual act of spitting turns the tables on this discourse. *It was not the Pharisees who needed protection from the sinfulness of the blind man, but it was the blind man who needed protection from the rest of the spiritually sick culture.* The blind man, for the first time, begins the Sabbath of his week truly renewed and worshiping freely in a new way than he ever had before.

Now I am not suggesting that we leave church on the lookout for people trying to lay curses upon us through the casting of the evil eye. But the Good News is that God spits before us as children, and offers us protection from the spiritual forces of principalities, powers, and spiritual wickedness in high places. We often have no conception of how much we are being protected and cared for, at any given time. We love the words of the 23rd Psalm, but we do not often really believe those words in deeply affective ways in terms of the protection offered to us in the words "The Lord is my shepherd—your rod and your staff, they comfort me."

And this is not to say that we should not work, as individuals, or as a church, or as a country or world community to help those who are in need, because so often our first reaction to tragedy or disaster—or even bad luck—is to look for some spiritual reason why God has ceased to protect the victims of earthquakes, or tsunamis, or even random acts of human evil. Because we have the protection much of the time does not mean that God has turned on others when bad things happen; just as the Pharisees wanted to blame the blind man's parents for his blindness. We should remember that our story of John involves two men that are more or less homeless and poor—Jesus and the blind man— against the Pharisees, who may not have been rich, but they had the luxury and the means to be out looking for people to tattle on. They had the luxury in their temple to focus their attention away from God in their preparation for the Sabbath to imposing their strict doctrine on others, and kicking people out instead of inviting new people in.

And even while it is easy for us to say that we don't give the "evil eye" to others, we should recall that it is not that long ago that it was a mainstream idea to blame AIDS victims for their disease as a disease that is from their sins. And as children (from heterosexual parents) began to be born with HIV, the discourse focused then upon the sins of the children's parents. This is not all that different than the Pharisees' accusations of the blind man.

We are now seeing our culture go through this shift when it comes to tobacco-induced cancers, and perhaps even to cellular-phone-induced brain tumors, and the way in which we talk about childhood and adult obesity. Or even the way some Christians have politicized the HPV vaccine that modern science has developed to protect women from cervical cancer. For those of us who are exposed to, or are close to anyone exposed to, or who has died from these physical problems, it's easy to point the finger at the one who is suffering, when we know these diseases are just as much social, societal, and spiritual as they are physical. Often we have no other way to think about these issues other than to place blame on someone sometime using our faith as a weapon for this blame, when we should instead use our faith to open the door for compassion and understanding from the divine source whose "goodness and mercy follow me all the days of my life."

The actual praise of God occurs not only outside of the temple in this story but by individuals who were not welcomed in the temple. So while we may praise God for comfort and protection, it is also necessary for us within the church to consider our own blindness and our own sight, and ask whether we give the evil eye to new people or outsiders, and finally appear before Jesus in such a way that he will spit on the ground before us, too.

Silent but Violent!

Psalm 31:9-16; Philippians 2:5-11; Matthew 21:1-17 (Lent 4)

Jesus arrives at the holy city of Jerusalem, a city that is believed to be the center of the universe by Jews, and he enters riding a donkey, and is welcomed into the city as a king with palms waving in the air. We should recall that while Jesus is given a king's welcome, the folks welcoming him into the city were many who betrayed Jesus in the end. But it would be a little bit of a mistake if we blamed the crowd entirely for Jesus' death; in fact, if we look into what was happening in this scene of scripture we are given new clues as to just how this story of Palm Sunday is connected to the crucifixion of Jesus, which happens just a few days later.

Part of the deal the Jews had with their Passover celebration was that the Roman governor would process into the city and demand a kind of worship to acknowledge the civic religion of the state, a religion that worshipped the Emperor. So long as the Jews complied with this practice, they could worship freely however they wanted, and so often the conflicts between the Roman Empire and the Jews were evoked as a result of the Jews' refusal to compromise in worshiping the idols of the empire. It's likely that the point of the palms in this story was that the date of the Roman procession to demand worship of the Empire and its gods coincided with the pagan holiday of the Festival of the Entry of the Tree, where a palm tree would have been carried through the city.

So Jesus processes into the city, following the Roman politician, probably on purpose, as a *parody* of the idol-worship of the Empire. What is interesting about the way that the Bible presents this story is that while this story was originally written in Greek, the word "Hosanna" is a foreign word from the

Aramaic language, and it means "Save us!" The Jews yelled this foreign word at the procession—*hosanna!*—of the Empire into the city, to give the appearance that they were worshiping the state gods, *while* they were really insulting the state gods. Waving the palm branches, they fanned the processing governor and symbols of the Emperor with their pagan symbols of worship, condemning the Roman ruler and their military who marched with them, condemning them by making a mockery of the Roman religion.

This reminds me of a famous Ethiopian proverb that goes like this: *When the great king passes by, the wise peasant bows deeply, and farts.*[1] In other words, the treatment of the processional that the Empire required through the city was turned into an *insult*, without the Romans having any idea of what they were *really* saying or gesturing. The cheering of the crowd made fun of the Romans and their pagan worship. And the parody continues with Jesus processing like a king, on a donkey, with the sick and the poor following him. It was all a big joke for many of them, insofar as the situation might be thought of as a "joke," and they believed that the joke was on the Empire.

But then the tone of the procession immediately changes as Jesus arrives to the heart of Jewish religious life, the center of the universe, the Temple. Now, the crowd could tolerate mocking the Roman Emperor, but Jesus then gives his final sermon. We should remember that Jesus' first sermon, the Sermon on the Mount, was directed at the poor living in the countryside and its villages. Now Jesus preaches to the rich and those who are the most religious at the center of society, that they have made the temple the opposite of anything godly. Jesus overturns the money changers' tables and enters the Temple.

And once he is inside the temple, the poor and the sick entered the temple and were given hope and healed. And then the priests heard the children continue the cry of the word, "Hosanna," directed at Jesus, but this time the word "Hosanna" was not a mockery, but it was genuine: it was a cry, meaning, "Lord, save us." But for those who held power in the temple, they now realized that Jesus not only made a mockery of the Empire but he now made a mockery of the priests.

*

It's fair to say that Pontius Pilate, the local ruling governor for the Roman Empire, saw this happen and understood that Jesus was good for neither the priests nor for Rome, and perhaps began to understand that the Roman Empire was being made a fool of as the peasants bowed in the streets, waved their palms, and secretly passed gas. Jesus, who was no real threat to Rome in a military sense, exposed the hypocrisy of his own leaders, who had sold out to Rome, and made a mockery of the Roman Empire. Jesus had to go.

But the most striking image that I have of Jesus from the whole ordeal is that the people who made a mockery of the Empire were *using* Jesus to make a political statement, but then the mockery turned on them. And as it happens, Jesus' mockery of the priests was quite serious. He might have processed in silently and gently on a donkey, but then he violently erupts and rebels against those who had financially benefitted from the temple. And then he goes into the temple and begins a new ministry without the permission or oversight of the priests.

Jesus did not replace the false gods of Rome with the mainstream religion of the Jews; rather, he walked into the empty temple and out of the absence of God and the absence of life from the temple, Jesus enacts new life. Jesus brings about hope in a place that was believed to be stagnant and dead. Jesus, who is portrayed as a madman, *going crazy*, overthrew the money changers who prevented real change from happening in the culture, while doing business at the foot of the temple; Jesus blasphemes the practicing religious and businessmen of his time and then *walks into the temple and strikes up his funeral ritual* for the ways of life of the past. By burying the past behind him, Jesus then brings about a New Creation Now Occurring in the new ritual of the physical sacrifice of himself, at the beginning of Holy Week. Jesus began to prepare those to whom he preached at the beginning of his ministry—the poor, the meek, the mourning, the peacemakers, and those who thirst for justice—for the most radical act of his life yet, namely, the coming of the death of God on the cross.

But the hope in all of this is that just as Jesus walks into the tomb of the temple and brings new life and hope out of its darkness and out of its absence, so also does Jesus *enter* the tomb and bring new life and new hope out of his own death.

And while there is hope for the new life that Christ brings with his crucifixion and resurrection, we have to ask whether there is hope for us. Is it possible for us to take these tombs and broken vessels of our bodies, and of our selves, and the tombs of our cars, and our jobs, and our families, and our communities, and the gravestones and sepulchers of God that is the church as we know it in our time, and sing a new song of New Creation, one that inspires the sick and the lonely and the oppressed? How can we live our lives with such ultimate joy that our children will reverse the cries of mockery from the crowd—*hosanna!*—into proclamations of new life and resurrection?

How can we do justice in the world in such a way that turns the social order around, where the last truly are first and the first truly are last, if we might find a way to proclaim that our lives, and our daily routines, and our churches have served the Lord of This Age for long enough, and it is now time to invite the Christ who is God poured out for us all into our hearts, and into our flesh, so that we too may follow Jesus in his walk of crucifixion, and sacrifice, and death? Do we have faith enough to believe that the more we are hated by the world, the more we embody ourselves with Christ in his descent into hell, that we might become part of the New World enacting all around us, working toward the return of Christ?

These are the powerful questions that lie before all of us, and our society, and the church in our present day and age. *Now* we must choose for ourselves whether we will make a mockery of our challenge, or will we answer the call to build together the Kingdom for Christ to return?

*

When we are children, thunderstorms are always special events, because they are at once exhilarating and frightening. In fact, I still like thunderstorms, especially in the calm and silence that often precedes them before the storm becomes realized. You have surely participated in the ritual, often done with children, of watching for lightning, and counting—*one-one-thousand, two-one-thousand, three-one-thousand*—for the sounds of thunder, to estimate how far away the lightning struck.

My friends, the Good News is that Easter is coming, and that Christ comes again. Today, this Palm Sunday, we hear the story of Jesus' reversal of the social order and his giving of himself in the beginning of his last days. In this story we are now beginning to see the flash of lightning of the greatest event in human history about to happen before us. We see the beginnings of a reversal of society that happened nearly 2,000 years ago and is still not fully realized. But even while we have seen the lightning, we know that thunder sometimes requires time, just as the light of the stars requires time to arrive to us.

The gloom and darkness, and silence and solitude of the coming days are looming upon us. Holy Week, when we truly experience it, is not an easy or comfortable experience. Living in our modern world with our technology, and our illusions of freedom in our country, and our lies of sophistication in our society all make it even more difficult, if not nearly impossible, for us to have any conception of the Great Reversals we are about to traverse through at the end of this Lenten journey. If we are to follow the footsteps of Jesus, the walk of Golgotha, then we must answer the call, for the call has happened, and the call is happening, whether we choose to answer this call or not.

Lightning and thunder require time.[2] The time is now upon us to be the thunder of the world, the thunder that shakes the ground and tears the veil of the temple curtain. Our call is now to speak and act into the absence and nothingness of the tombs all around us and reverse the course of history, and genuinely name the breath of emptiness that we all experience in our lives, as an absence that may now breathe new life. We must begin to pronounce the promise, a flash of lightning of which we have only previously known before as a rumor, and speak it genuinely, even if we must only *whisper* it on this Day of Palms: *Easter.*

The Season of Easter

Too Good to be True!

Colossians 3:1-4; Matthew 27:45-28:15 (Easter)

Earlier in this Sunday's worship service, I read Bear Wants More *by Jane Chapman and Karma Wilson during the children's message.*[1]

When was the last time something happened to you that was just too good to be true? Like finding out that the one you had a crush on also has a crush on you? Or that after searching for a long time, you finally got a job that you wanted? Or after years of waiting, your prayers are answered?

But we also live in a world where sometimes what could be believed to be too good to be true doesn't happen and we are just faced with a long line of bad luck.

And we can also conceive of the fact that when things do go our way, and when our prayers are answered, that we are rarely, if ever, satisfied when the things that we believe to be too good to be true actually happen. They might be "good" but we can always think of something better.

And we also can relate to times when what is believed to be too good to be true ends up being a big disappointment. Or even that what is too good to be true ends up being something we wish we had never encountered or desired before.

The problem that we have with our desire for tangible objects and for the consumption of things is that we always want more. There is almost always something that we want, and when we get it, we are on to the next thing, much like the story of the Bear in Jane Chapman and Karma Wilson's *Bear Wants More.*

The situation we are presented with in our scripture reading for this Easter Sunday is precisely about an event that is too good to be true. Jesus dies on the cross, and he offers a final gasp of desperation, or dereliction, from the cross, the disciples become afraid, and run away. A guard is placed to watch over Jesus' tomb to ensure that nothing strange happens, and then—we know the story—Jesus reappears, alive, to the women. The guards are, the scriptures tell us, so overcome that they shook and passed out, as if they had died, frozen in their tracks.

But the women are told not to be afraid, to tell the disciples that Jesus has returned. They are so overcome that they do just this, and then they encounter Jesus, and are so overwhelmed that they immediately leave to tell more people what has happened. What has happened is simply too good to be true. The truth of what has happened has become secondary to the goodness and overwhelming joy they were experiencing. The resurrection of Christ is *too good to be true.*

*

The characters that are often overlooked in this story include the guards who are placed to watch Jesus' grave. The religious leaders came to Pontius Pilate and requested that a guard be placed to watch the tomb to be sure no funny business happened. Since Pilate saw Jesus as a threat to the peace between his political control over the Jews, he agrees so as to keep them happy, and he sends several guards.

But when the angel appears at the grave, an earthquake happens, the stone is rolled away, and the soldiers' bodies convulsed, and, as the Bible says, they "became like dead men." What was happening around them was unbelievable, beyond their comprehension. But the women, who were mourning, and apparently frightened by these events, did not fall down as if they were dead. Instead, they are told that Jesus has been raised, which up until this point could only have been something that remained with them as an *imaginary* possibility, as something that would just be too good to be true. The Good News was something that was in fact *Good News* for the women, whereas the Good News of Easter could only be something bad for the soldiers, who failed in preventing any funny business from happening.

So the guards had to then answer to the priests, who conspire to make up a story that makes sense—that they fell asleep and the disciples stole the body of Jesus. The soldiers had to report the facts of what happened to someone, because they are interested only in doing their job, and now that it appears that they failed at their job, they can only respond to the facts by making up a false story that remains *within the realm of the possible*. The priests even conclude that their story will dupe Pilate and that the soldiers would then not get in trouble with him. To sweeten the situation, the priests even give the soldiers money to bribe them to tell the story exactly the way the priests wanted it to be heard.

What is interesting to me here is that the guards, who are interested in the facts, become, according to the scriptures, "like dead" when encountered with the resurrection of Christ. *A radical reversal is occurring here*: those who are mourning, and those who thirst for justice, that is, the women, are no longer walking in a death that ends like a dead-end, but instead, *in the death of Christ they are faced with a reality that is too good to be true*. The truth of the events no longer matters, because death, and burial, all become *relative* to a New World that is Now Occurring. Little would they understand that while they watched Jesus bleed to death a few days before, and listened to Jesus cry out in dereliction a bold statement of atheism, "My God, My God, why have you forsaken me"—that is, Jesus, as God, *renouncing* God on the cross—that through this death of God on the cross, life itself is now given *new life*, it is given new meaning.

To try to understand the resurrection as a factual sequence of events, as something that historically happened in the past, is something that is being done in churches all around the world on this Easter morning. The reality is that the conspiracy of the resurrection of Christ as simply a historical event of the past began on the first Easter Sunday, as this is what the guards tried to do when they awoke, as they began to make sense of what happened and tried to figure out what to do, and then they went to the priests, who could only make sense of the resurrection by denying that it had any reality at all. To the priests, it made no difference whether the resurrection happened or not, in fact, I suspect that they believed that it happened; yet they were far more interested in explaining what had happened, because this secret of the resurrection was just too good to be true.

I am convinced that by reducing the resurrection to an argument about history—which is what I would suspect you would hear in many churches today, on *this* Easter morning—is really no different than what the priests instructed the soldiers to tell Pontius Pilate on that *first* Easter morning. In fact, as some of you know I have been reading the holy text of Islam, the Qur'an, in the past few months, and I have always known that Muslims deny the resurrection of Christ, but I have been especially struck by the words of the Qur'an, which claims that neither the crucifixion nor the resurrection happened, but instead, the book teaches, the Christians "just imagined it," and that Christians "have no knowledge" about the end of Jesus' life; instead, we are "just guessing" about Easter (Sura 4:157). The Gospel of Matthew, at the conclusion of our reading today, said that the story the priests told the guards to say about Jesus "is still told" today, and I believe that this statement is *true*.

The reality is that we don't know exactly what historically happened on that first Easter Sunday morning, and if we do take a historical position we just create an argument. The Good News of *this* Easter is that we have a third option away from the argument about whether the resurrection happened or not as a fact: namely, this third option is the position of the women who encounter Christ in the garden, where the resurrection is too good to be true, and it's too good to be false. The return of Jesus enacts in us a call to step away from the downward spiral of our typical lives, and of our sufferings, and of our angers, and our mournings, and our injustices, and in this suffering, find *new life* and New Creation. When it's too good to be true, the absurdity of the resurrection calls us to joy. When it's too good to be true, we are led from our ordinary lives to something extra-ordinary.

*

A good question might be raised about the practicality of living out Easter, and what this might mean.

I think we can learn something from the children's book *Bear Wants More* by Jane Chapman and Karma Wilson. In the book, the bear comes out from his hibernation in his cave, and walks around the forest, meeting his other animal friends, and his hunger and desire for food leads him to eat, and eat, and eat. And while he is out getting food, some other friends are back at his cave getting ready to throw him a party. But when the bear returns, he has become so fat that he can't get in his cave anymore. The bear gets stuck, and his friends pry him out, and throw a party for him *outside* of the cave.

I like to think that if we are to find ourselves in the story of *Bear Wants More*, we're not really the bear, although we can see ourselves in the bear, always wanting more, and for some of us, getting so fat that we don't fit through the doorway of our caves anymore.

I would suggest that living the Easter life, the resurrection life, is being the friends for the bear, preparing food for the bear after he is out-on-the-town, in the forest, eating food that is not fulfilling. The bear came out of his cave and intends on returning to his cave.

Because we do not live in death, because Easter is just too good to be true, we meet our friends who are determined to live in their caves, or tombs, outside of their caves, and meet their basic needs. We seek those who are poor, and mourning, and downtrodden, and we feed them, we comfort them, and we work to dismantle the social powers that hold them in chains. And in doing so, we teach and proclaim that now it is spring, and a New Creation is blossoming all around us, and there is no longer any need to stay indoors, in our caves, and hibernate. We all know people who stay in their caves, or tombs, all year long, watching flickering shadows of the world on their walls, and never really venturing to see the new life that awaits them outside.

As a resurrection people, it's our job to stand by the tomb and proclaim that we have seen the resurrection, and it isn't just about making our life better, and it isn't about starting an argument about what has happened at the tomb of Christ, but instead it's about the life *that is better than life in the cave*, that *the un-resurrected life is not worth living*. That there is an abundance of new life outside of the tomb.

*

You have surely heard of the story about the minister, who, on Easter Sunday, decided to quiz the children during the children's sermon. He asked the children if they knew what day it was, and they looked at each other and answered, "Easter."

He then asked them what happened on Easter. One very astute child courageously spoke up and boldly proclaimed, "The stone rolled away from the big hole!"

The congregation chuckled at how boldly the little child said this, and then the pastor said, "But then what happened?" The same child raised her hand, and the pastor said, "How 'bout we ask someone else to talk?"

A little boy looked up and asked the pastor a question, "You mean what happened after Jesus came out of the hole?" The pastor nodded and said, "Yes, do you know what happened then?"

The little boy said, "Jesus came out of the big hole."

The pastor praised the boy: "Very good!"

But then the boy added: "And when he saw his shadow, there was six more weeks of winter."

This is my point. Easter gives us the opportunity to step out of our tombs, and to help others in coming into the light outside of their caves and encourage them against the choice of letting the moment of Easter be sealed in the tomb of a dusty story of long ago. We must proclaim that the resurrection of Christ is not only Good News for Jesus, as the one raised from the grave on the first Easter, and Good News is not only Good News for the women mourning by the tomb on the first Easter, in taking the next big step of history by proclaiming that this Easter, *our Easter*, is too Good to be true. It is stepping boldly out of our own tombs, basking in the light, and joining Christ in our own transcending of "life" and of "death."

For if we are bearing the cross of Christ on our journey, and fulfill our baptism as being baptized in Christ's life and his death, we too are invited to cry from the cross in our darkest moments, "My God, my God, why have you forsaken me?" And out of the deep and empty cave of our cries of dereliction and abandonment, we may have hope for ourselves, and for others, that these dry bones may find new life, and we must proclaim boldly this New Life, which is truly too good to be true, loudly into every cave where there is death and despair, for this Good News is not just a resurrection of Jesus, but a resurrection of ourselves, as we walk out of this church this morning, smashing behind us the chains and tombs that hold us back from living New Life. For on this Sunday, this Easter, we are empowered to enact the New Creation with every person we encounter and touch, and ask those around us, "Why are you weeping?" Our presence alone, as living New Life in Christ, is now reason alone to reverse the course of the world.

Where's the Death Certificate?

Psalm 16:5-11; 1 Peter 1:3-9; John 20:19-31 (Easter 2)

This sermon was preached shortly after the military assassination of Osama bin Laden (May 2, 2011), amidst growing public outcry by a myriad of conservative American political voices regarding President Barack Obama's citizenship. Billboards were cropping up in the area, reading, "Where's the Birth Certificate?"[1] This was all a convenient background for preaching the story of Doubting Thomas.

I was sitting in a hospital waiting room with one of our church members, who is not here today, while another of our church members was in surgery. Broadcast on the flat-screen television set in the waiting room was the unending discussion and reporting of every single detail, from every possible journalistic and rhetorical angle, of Osama bin Laden's death. While it is clear that we should be asking about the legality of what happened and about the status of our U.S. allegiances with Pakistan at this point, so much of the public curiosity since bin Laden's death has been centered around photographs taken of his dead corpse. And this is because apparently many Americans don't believe that he is dead.

And I shouldn't be surprised, since one of my own family members immediately informed me that he didn't believe that Osama was dead, either. What we now have around us is a situation where the American public distrusts its elected leadership so harshly that nothing that our leadership does is ever believed. It's telling that within hours of President Obama releasing his birth certificate that public voices on our local radio station claimed that they released the birth certificate strategically because Michelle Obama could not stand the fact that the royal wedding in England was taking international attention off of her! We should also not dismiss the fact that our top elected leadership is black to be a contributing factor as to why white America doesn't trust the government; racism is clearly a factor in what is happening all around us.

But in our Bible reading for today, we encounter the story of "doubting" Thomas. Jesus visits the disciples, who were afraid, following news of the resurrection. Jesus greets them, saying, "Peace to you," which is what we say when we pass the peace in church every Sunday, and then he commands them to "receive the Holy Spirit," and he starts breathing on them, offering them forgiveness.

Why would Jesus start breathing on them and offering them forgiveness? Jesus doing this is a ritual re-creation of Yom Kippur, which is the Jewish day of atonement and forgiveness. The disciples, who had betrayed Jesus, were afraid for their lives, and the Bible says that they were afraid of what the priests would do to them when they learned that Jesus had risen from the dead, but they were probably also afraid of what Jesus might do, too. And it's telling, then, that Jesus immediately offers them forgiveness and offers a fresh start.

Jesus is also beginning a new era of history. By breathing the Holy Spirit, we should recognize that this Jesus, who returns from the grave, is *not the same as before*. He is different. He is post-grave, post-Hell, and post-tomb. A lot has happened to Jesus in a very short amount of time. And by Jesus breathing the Spirit onto the disciples, now forgiven, they too are changed with Jesus, and thereby a new era of human history is being enacted, as the Holy Spirit is beginning its outpouring onto humanity, which will culminate later into the Holy Spirit pouring out onto the church on the Day of Pentecost.

Thomas is not present while the Holy Spirit is being breathed out by Jesus, and, even seeing Jesus in person about a week later, Thomas doesn't believe it. A good question here is what is it he didn't believe? Jesus offers Thomas peace, and allows him to insert his fingers into the holes in his body.

Very often we are taught that Thomas did not believe that Jesus had risen from the dead, and the conclusion is that those who doubt Easter are denying what is plainly true in front of them. But it seems to me that Thomas believes that Jesus is alive, obviously, but rather Thomas just doesn't believe that Jesus had died. Until he sees the wounds and dismembered body of Jesus, flesh that should be dead, now alive, Thomas does not believe in the death of Jesus. It is the death of Jesus that now seems unimaginable since he sees Jesus alive, because how could anything alive also be dead? What Thomas didn't understand at that point was that when it comes to God, as Jesus, "life" and "death" become relative terms. They take on new meaning. Jesus had been raised, and in the Holy Spirit, so also may Thomas be raised as well, and belief in Jesus causes us to move beyond the literal and into the spiritual meaning of "life" and "death."

*

If you're a baseball fan like me, you can often relate history to baseball, or you begin to connect historical events to baseball. For instance, I had tickets to see the Chicago Cubs play the St. Louis Cardinals at Wrigley Field on September 11, 2001, a game that was cancelled that day. Shortly thereafter I was at the Chicago White Sox game against the New York Yankees at what is now U.S. Cellular Park, or the newer Comiskey Stadium, on the South Side of Chicago.

That game was the first baseball game played by a New York team after 9/11, and the tenor and ceremony that took place with that baseball game is unlike anything I have ever seen. Before the game numerous first responders from New York City were honored, Mayor Giuliani gave a speech, and "God Bless America" on that day became a common hymn for baseball games ever since. The display of patriotism against the horror of

the World Trade Center's collapse just a week before caused me
to experience a tremendous sense of dread, a dread that we
would go to war blindly. In fact, I even wrote an op-ed article for
the *Chicago Weekly News*, a weekly newspaper for which I wrote
an occasional column, about this experience shortly after it
happened.

And late last Sunday night I was watching the Phillies game
go into extra innings, watching the crowd at Citizens Bank Park
care less about the Phillies' eventual fourteen-inning loss to the
Mets as news of Osama bin Laden's death overtook the crowd.[1]

While there is no question that bin Laden was a bad person, a
man whose hands were stained with blood, a man who sucked
our country into a state of international war, a war that cannot
ever really be won and where victories and losses are difficult to
identify, I experienced a similar kind of dread over the crowd's
reaction and patriotism as I experienced at Comiskey Park about
ten years before.

It is abundantly ringing all around us that we live in a culture
of death. We live in a culture that celebrates death and celebrates
the demise of others. The rejoicing over the death of a human
being, any human being, suggests that bin Laden didn't "win" or
"lose," but that his death is just another death in a society gone
backwards. He was a major player in this society at one time, but
his death might give us a false sense of victory or an illusion that
life has triumphed over death, that good has defeated evil. The
fact is, bin Laden is not a casualty of a war he did not begin, but
he has been a casualty of the same society in which we are partic-
ipants and victims.

Amid calls to see images of the dead body of bin Laden we
could only see mirror images of ourselves. In gory photographs
we could only understand the work of our own hands and our
inability to grapple with the cultural and international situations
that we ourselves simultaneously cause and attack.

Do we, like Thomas, need to stick our hands into the dead

body of bin Laden to accept that he is dead? Does the absence of the body really incite a belief that he has survived death? It is interesting, if not telling, that the most conservative Americans who doubt the death of bin Laden share this belief with a few extremist Muslims, that Osama bin Laden is still alive. Or will we finally realize that his death points to our tragic state of affairs which believes that his life or his death means something beyond the base tragedy of our situation?

If we have received the Spirit, if we have been greeted with Christ in peace, we must understand that, as Jesus taught, the *dead bury their own dead*. And in the death-culture in which we live, this *necrophilial*, death-lusting culture, we do not always seek proof of life, but we are obsessed with proof of death, because this is all we can truly know. And when we do search out proof of life, it is to facilitate our culture of death. Just as for many Americans, the President's "Certificate of Live Birth" from the state of Hawaii was insufficient proof that he was born where he was born, the reality is that we live in a state of Live Death.

*

In our other scripture reading from 1 Peter today, St. Peter writes that God's "great mercy has given us a new birth into a living hope through the resurrection of Jesus Christ from the dead, and into an inheritance that is imperishable, undefiled, and unfading." If we are led by Christ into a Kingdom journey that calls us into imperishability, and an undefiled and unfading world, why do we celebrate so loudly the perishability, fading away, and defiling of others, even while these celebrations point to our own finitude?

The Good News is that we do this because we are not yet fully molded into the New Creation to which we are challenged. We do not live in such a way that truly seeks life over death, except when it is our life and our own pleasure that we seek. We do not live in a true joy, except for the kind of joy that reduces our current state of affairs to games or end-results that justify games, *or wars*, that should have never happened or are deeply immoral in themselves. We celebrate outcomes when they are easy and cheap—and I would contend that while the price we paid as a nation for the hunt for Osama bin Laden was clearly financially expensive (some saying today that the cost was close to one trillion dollars)—the spiritual payoff of putting bullets through a man that was already spiritually dead demonstrates that our death overpowered his death. It is far more difficult to seek out life, and promote life, than simply rejoice in death.

In our Psalm reading for today, Psalm 16, David writes: "Therefore my heart is glad, and my soul rejoices, my body also rests secure, for you do not give me up to Sheol, or let your faithful one see the Pit. You show me the path of life, in your presence there is fullness of joy; in your right hand are pleasures forevermore." "Sheol" is the Hebrew word for the afterlife in the early Jewish religion, though it is sometimes seen as a word for "hell." Sheol is perhaps more accurately a word for the state of death in which the dead reside. The Psalm teaches us that joy brings us beyond simple conceptions of life and death, to a "fullness" of joy, in the "path of life."

My point is this. If we live in a perpetual culture of death, it is Christ who calls us out of the tombs and graveyards where we constantly live. And if the world itself, and by this I mean the whole of human culture, is a world of death, it isn't like we can just emigrate to somewhere that is more life-loving. We can only try to kindle a new light of hope for life in the darkness of death, even while spring is happening around us, even while celebrations of death occur everywhere, while it is so difficult to convince the death-culture that there is a better life.

Easter is a day that Christ calls us to come out of the tombs, but as the season of Easter continues we must understand that while we may exit our own tombs, we begin to realize that the world itself is a tomb into which we must bring new life. It's not enough just to live Easter for ourselves. Instead, we invite the dead to place their dead fingers into life that is now beyond death, to begin to believe that there is life beyond life, and life beyond death. On the first day of Easter we encounter new life as astonishment, and now that we have overcome the shock of Easter, we must now accept that if we do not live Easter in a magnetic way that is a triumph over death, our Easter simply becomes another hymn in the over-arching liturgy of death that is struck up everywhere throughout the world.

This Place Stinks!

Genesis 28:10-19; Luke 24:13-35 (Easter 3)

The story of the Emmaus walk is well known: It is the evening of the first Easter, and two of the disciples, one of them may have been female, are walking toward Emmaus, and Jesus appears to them, but they do not recognize him. They share a meal together and as soon as they see him eating, they recognize Jesus, and then he suddenly vanishes from them.

One little-known fact about this story is that it takes place at the same place where the vision of Jacob's ladder occurs, which is identified as "Luz" or "Bethel" in the scriptures. The vision is of a ladder from earth leading up to heaven, with angels ascending, then descending from the ladder, all while Jacob is resting with his head on a rock as a pillow.

The symbolism of Jesus reappearing and vanishing in the same location of the vision of Jacob's ladder is a difficult question, and nothing in the Bible is ever purely coincidental.

When Jacob wakes up from his dream, the two things he says, in the words of the King James Version of the Bible, are telling. First, he says, "surely the Lord is in this place, and I knew it not." Second, Jacob then woke up, looked around at how awful the place was, the sort of place where you could only use a rock as your pillow, and said while he was afraid, "how dreadful this place is!" Again, the place was called "Luz" or "Bethel," which is the same place known as Emmaus when the Gospel of Luke was written and codified later.

As you probably know, our church is physically located in Bethel Township, even though our mailing address is Lebanon, Pennsylvania. We should recall that it is in Bethel, in the countryside, in the Bible where Jesus briefly appears, even for a fleetingly short time, and where Jacob has an intense vision followed by him waking up and saying, the Lord is in this place, and later, *man, this place stinks!*

And, quite honestly, this place does stink, as some of you know, for instance: our first spring here at the church; one time we were coming to church for a meeting while it was "spreadin' season" around the church, and my son yelled, "Yuck! What's that smell!" We told him that it was cow poop. And he said, as only a two year old can say, "That must be one sick cow!" But even while the place might stink, the "Lord is in this place."

I am often reminded of Mother Teresa's memoirs, where she wrote that she had this powerful religious experience as a teenager, and the rest of her life she never felt anything of God ever again. In fact the absence of God from her was so painfully powerful that it overwhelmed her. The only way she could respond to this absence was to serve the poorest of the poor and inspire others on her Christian walk.[1]

In her memoirs, which she ordered to be destroyed at her death, so instead they were published, she wrote to the claim that many made while she was still alive that she was a saint, that "if I were to become a saint, I could only be a saint of darkness," as one who only briefly felt God for a moment in her life, only saw one brief spark of light, but spent the rest of her life yearning for more but never felt anything ever again.

The fact is that most of our lives are spent in the absence of God—we don't typically feel God all the time, and some of us never feel God's presence. For me, I don't ever feel God working through me in the present, but when I reflect and look back I believe that God has guided me and worked through me in various times and places, sometimes at times when I felt most lost and most abandoned.

So the world might stink around us, but often we are called, like Jacob, to look around and notice that the terrible place where we might be located is also a place where we experience God in brief, fluttering moments. And often by the time we recognize the presence of God with us, the presence becomes suddenly absent, just like Jesus in Emmaus on the first Easter.

You may have heard the story about the little boy who sees a farmer hauling manure on the tractor in his village, and the boy asks the farmer, "where are you going to put all of that manure?"

The farmer said, "I'm going to spread this all over my strawberries!"

The little boy looked up at the famer and replied, "I thought around here we just put sugar and cream on our strawberries!"

How we interpret the divine at work in our lives is often a matter of perspective, whether we're willing to not only listen to the Spirit whispering in our ears, and speaking through dreaming visions, but more importantly to wake up and state plainly that this place around us *stinks*. When Jacob realized this, he built an altar, marking the spot where he once experienced a vision but no longer experienced God. As a historical event, Jesus, as God, would literally walk that spot hundreds of years later, but Jacob would not experience God there ever again. Yet he played an important role as a prophet that led to many more experiencing God in his time and later on in history.

So here we find ourselves today in this area named after this place, "Bethel." Sometimes it may stink, and sometimes it might seem like the farmland and the mission field are more rocks than soil, but this place is where we occasionally experience the divine, even if it is only in brief moments, and we may only be faithful by going out and building the Kingdom, even as we experience despair, sadness, or even fear as we mourn for the loss of the past, because God is always making all things New.

Good News to the World the Church has Hurt

Psalm 66:8-20; 1 Peter 3:13-22; John 14:15-21 (Easter 6)

One of the most important things I have learned about counseling and being a pastor was something I learned while I was serving as a prison chaplain intern at Indiana State Prison, and I was thinking about this while I was driving by the town where the prison is, just north of Route 80, on my drive to Chicago two weeks ago. The nun who supervised my internship wrote a book on grieving, and she taught those of us whom she supervised to ask to ourselves the people whom we encounter what they are grieving.[1] We are all grieving something, we're always in a state of mourning for something or another. Sometimes we're not aware of what we're mourning, as in the case of the times when we're in the dumps, or at times when what we're grieving is so present around us that we have become blind to it. And at other times it is clear what we're mourning, as in the time after we experience the death of someone close to us.

And as we all have had the experience of losing someone to death, we also know that it is our faith that often guides us through the loss, and our faith gives us hope that we will one day be reunited with the one who has left us but that our shared faith makes our lives better and makes our lives more meaningful. Our shared faith is a place where, as Jesus says in our scripture reading this morning, we "abide." Living our faith together makes us touch more lives as a community, and it makes the loss of one of us even greater. But the loss of life underscores the intimacy, the empathy, and the brotherly love that can be experienced across generations within the church, especially in a world where generations are separated more and more from each other.

We should pay attention to the context in which Jesus' speech from the Gospel of John, our reading this morning, was given. Jesus promises that he will remain with his disciples forever, that he will not leave them, that he will not leave us orphaned, and because *he lives* he will abide, or live, in us and that we will abide in him. And he promises that the Holy Spirit will come upon his faithful. There is a lot of theology behind these words, but the *context* is also important. The Gospel of John was written during a time when the Jews were being persecuted, millions of them had been killed at the hands of Roman soldiers, and the small Christian group was separated from the more dominant Jewish religion from which it came. At the time these words were written down by John it's also quite likely that more non-Jews were becoming Christians than Jewish-born individuals.

In other words, they were a small cult, a small group of people that were likely fairly diverse, but they were all individuals who had not just joined a new denomination of their local religion, they were joining something entirely new and something that would have been considered offensive or abhorrent by their families and the dominant culture. They were considered heretics and blasphemers. In the story, the disciples were covenant-breakers and were considered apostate from their communities and their families. They may be mourning the coming departure of Jesus, but they were also mourning and grieving the family and community ties that they had given up to follow Jesus. They were likely no longer welcome in the temple, might not have been able to participate or witness weddings and funerals, and they may have not been allowed to receive a proper burial by their family. But while their relationship with Jesus was stronger and beyond all of these things, they probably still mourned for these losses.

So when Jesus says "abide in me and I will abide in you," Jesus was speaking to individuals who were at least spiritually homeless and were probably physically homeless. And after what had happened, with Jesus rising from the dead, they couldn't go home even if they wanted to. And we should remember that most of the disciples were killed for preaching the Gospel.

The longer I am a pastor and the more I talk to adults about their faith, the more I am convinced that even though people are not killed for their beliefs in our community, many of us have experienced a similar kind of spiritual homelessness or have been hurt or abused by the church in some way at one time or another. For some of us, that hurtfulness has come by way of an abuse of power of a pastor or someone else in leadership in the church. For others, we got too involved and too wrapped up in a church and it overwhelmed us and burned us out. I know that a few of us in this congregation have experienced cult-like behavior in former faith communities, where our money, our medical decisions, and even sexual relationships were dictated by the church or its pastor.

Those hurtful experiences and banishments remain with us and sometimes still shape how we act or behave. The fact is that to authentically be a Christian today is to be a Christian living in exile, that if we are too comfortable in our institutions and in our faith situations, if we have never really been challenged, if we have never been offended by the Gospel—we are serving the church and ourselves, and not the *Christ who redeems us.*

That sometimes we need to stand up for Jesus and walk with the Lord out of an institution or community is a moment where we may look back upon that moment and yearn for the togetherness and unity which we once felt, and feel tenuously confident that the time to move on is a way of protecting the integrity of our walk in Christ. Here I am not talking about churches leaving a denomination, many of our Lutheran congregations are doing that around us, but I am talking about situations where the church itself acts to protect its own borders, or leaders act to preserve their own sovereignty, and thus disclose a very narrow understanding of the *Christ who sustains us* in this pluralistic and diverse world.

I believe in Christianity not because of the absolutes which the religion imposes on religious ideas, offering borders across which I am not to color, but I believe *because* Christianity is a religion of crossing borders and going into new frontiers—both geographical and spiritual. I believe in Christ as my Lord because he promises to abide with us, and we in him, and not in the worship of a static and fixed sky-God who wants us to live in the Stone Age. I believe in Christianity precisely because it is a religion of exile, it is a religion of blasphemers and heretics who speak out against injustice, even and especially when it is unpopular and when the injustice is perpetuated by the dominant culture and the predominant religion.

Our confidence, and our Good News, is that if Christianity is a border-crossing faith, it is one where if we bear our own cross and walk with Christ, and invite Christ to abide in us, we enter into exile as a community that can truly change the world, for it is a world of hurt and grieving in which we live. And the more we look at the hurt the more we can begin to understand; as atheists love to remind us how much the church often creates and causes the hurt in the world. Bearing the cross, crossing borders, and crossing-out bad religion leads us into a faith of the Holy Spirit, where new languages, of faith identities, and states of living may be achieved.

Jesus' first followers in the Bible were not the rich, they were not those who had authority in the Temple, they were not the varsity athletes, and they weren't the highly educated. They were the sick, those who worked with their hands, the disabled, and others who were marginalized by some aspect of their culture. The same is often true today, as a church of misfits, exiled people, and hurting and grieving disciples. The first disciples were willing to speak truth to power, to reverse the course of history, and to make significant sacrifices, including their lives, for the God of History to enact anew into the resurrection and ministry of Christ. They bore their crosses and crossed their borders. The challenge to us today is to ask ourselves, "why are we grieving?", just as Jesus asked the women in the garden on the first Easter, and to walk into the warmth of the sun shining on a new day, as a church in exile, a church ready to bear the cross for others, and a Holy Spirit people prepared to speak the new language of those scores of people around us desperately searching, yearning, and grieving for the New Hope which Christ alone may offer.

The World has Already Ended!

Psalm 68:1-10, 32-35; 1 Peter 4:12-14, 5:6-11;
Luke 24:44-52 / John 17:1-11 (Ascension Sunday/Easter 7)

A few weeks ago, the Christian radio evangelist Harold Camping once again predicted the end of the world, and most observations are that the end of the world did not happen on May 21. We should remember that the same man, Harold Camping, predicted that the world would end previously on May 21, 1988, and on September 7, 1994.[1]

There's been a lot of talk about the end of the world in the media in the weeks leading up to May 21, and some since then. You may have heard the story about the pastor who asks those in his adult Bible study about what they would do if they found out that judgment day was coming four weeks from today.

The first woman said that she would go into the center of town and witness to everyone who would hear about the Gospel.

The pastor rose his eyebrows and said, "very good!"

The second man said that he would spend as much time with his family and closest friends, including and especially those with whom he had had big disagreements for years, to make amends and to publicly repent for his wrongdoing to them.

The pastor, knowing the man's background replied, "that sounds like a good idea."

But then the third person, a man, said, "I would move in with my mother-in-law for those four last weeks."

Perplexed a little, the pastor asked, "is she sick?"

The man said, "No, pastor, but living with the old bat would make those four weeks the longest four weeks of my life!"

*

On my drive to Chicago a few weeks ago I was kind of surprised how many billboards, signs on barns, and bumper stickers there were saying that the world was going to end on May 21, 2011. While driving home from Chicago to Pittsburgh on that fated day, I listened on the religious radio stations, ridiculing the prediction that nothing had happened, and I have since been following Camping's response. I actually heard someone report that the preacher had killed himself, but I knew this wouldn't have happened, because he had made these predictions before. He is now saying that God has begun his final judgment of the world on May 21 and the rapture and the destruction of the world will happen on October 21.

You may have heard stories of individuals and families selling everything that they had in preparation for May 21. CNN reported last week that some left their life savings to Harold Camping's radio station, which had a total of $18 million in donations in 2009, and apparently family members of a deceased woman are suing to get money back from the radio station.

The New York Daily News reported shortly before May 21 came and went that a new business began, called "Eternal Earth-Bound Pets," which guarantees that for a fee, a "confirmed atheist" will care for your pet in the event that a Christian is taken away by the rapture.[2] Because someone has to ask the question, what happens to Fido if Jesus comes again? What happens to Christians' pets who are left behind? Their website's tagline is "the next best thing to pet salvation in a post rapture world" and according to the newspaper, they have over 250 clients.

We all know that predictions of the end of the world are nothing new; in fact, we also all know the fable of Chicken Little or "Henny Penny," who is hit in the head by an acorn and concludes that the sky is falling. We should recall that the most famous American prediction of the end of the world was in 1843 and 1844 by a New York man named William Miller. He later changed his prediction to October 22, 1844, and of course Jesus did not return while thousands of people gathered together along with thousands more in their churches around the country. Many gave away their possessions and then had to rebuild their lives. The event is called by historians "The Great Disappointment"— many of those bewildered by Jesus' failure to return became Quakers and the rest became the foundations for the churches today known as Adventists and Jehovah's Witnesses.[3]

Today is Ascension Sunday, the Sunday before Pentecost; Jesus' ascension into the sky is one of the more perplexing concepts in the Christian faith. Jesus is carried away into the spiritual temple of the heavens to be with the Father. But what does this mean for us?

The theologian Bruce Epperly explains to us that the ascension is a matter of perspective. In other words, "rising to the clouds gives us a broader perspective on our lives and the planet," that our Christian faith is not really about getting a ticket into heaven—you will notice that the Bible actually states nowhere that those who die immediately go to heaven—but instead, the ascension is about following Christ as much as we can while we are alive. But if Christ is now in heaven, it is upon us to pull Christ back down to earth. Epperly advises that we should listen to the words of the Lord's prayer, words we know so well that we hardly know them at all, that we pray for things to be "on earth as it is in heaven." Following the way of the cross, which is to live our baptism, is to heave down the ascending Christ, to reverse the course of history which allows God to handle the business of the world and us to be complacent in the downward spiral of history. Reversing course is taking up our own cross and living and doing justice in a way that makes the world that is largely and seemingly absent of Christ to have sparks of the divine and to open windows for the spirit all around us.[4]

To this end, the ascension also indicates a new age of history for humanity. Jesus coming into the world marked the beginning of a new page of history, and Jesus' absence now begins something new. The age of Pentecost begins shortly after the ascension. The point is that with the disappearance of Christ in the world, and the coming of the age of the Holy Spirit on the Day of Pentecost, every day and every moment of every day begins something new, as stated in the book of Revelation, "Behold, I am making all things new." Every moment of every day someone in the world is being born, someone is dying, someone is getting married, someone is healed, and someone is being baptized. New worlds are being created all of the time. All of these life events take on new meaning within the newness that Christ offers.

But aside from the extraordinary events of birthing, dying, baptizing, healing, and marrying are the ordinary moments that comprise the rest of our lives. Christ might be made known in explicit ways through the rituals and ceremonies of baptisms and weddings and funerals, but it is the moments and experiences outside of church where the newness of Christ is truly made known to us and those around us. Finding Christian joy in every aspect of our lives, even those that are plain and ordinary, is what truly brings about a new heaven and a new earth.

It is with this belief that I name the mistake of Harold Camping not so much that the world ended on May 21, but that the world ending is not a once and done event, but the end of the world is an ongoing event. The world did end on May 21, but it ended thousands and millions of times over, and it also began millions of times over on that day. And Christ is doing the same every second of every moment of every day. And those who have ridiculed Harold Camping and his end-times followers are also wrong because the world did end, just not in the way that he said it would. Similarly, today we witnessed a baptism, which is a symbol of the dying of the old and the birthing of the new, and in doing so we renew and reaffirm our own baptisms.

Living the baptized life requires us to live and die with Christ, to come down to earth and to rise up to the heavens, to make holy the things of this world and to make earthly the joys of heaven, as we live in wait for the hour of Christ's actual and full return and the resurrection of the dead.

Pentecost and the Season after Pentecost

Pentecost: Speaking in Burps

Psalm 104:24-34, 35b; 1 Corinthians 12:3b-13;
John 7:37-39; Acts 2:1-21 (Day of Pentecost)

The Day of Pentecost is the birthday of the church, a day which Spirit pours onto all flesh, thereby making all flesh *new flesh*. Humanity is changed to the point that a new language is now being spoken.

The Day of Pentecost is foreshadowed by Jesus' prediction in John 7, where Jesus promises that his followers will be filled through the Spirit like "living waters." What does this mean?

I have always just assumed that the phrase "living waters" means water that is flowing naturally in a creek or in a river. But if you observe water that is *living*, it is filled with bubbles and air. This is the water Jesus says the thirsty will drink upon receiving the Spirit.

You can ask any teenage boy to demonstrate that if you drink some soda or carbonated water, you burp, and you can sing or talk while you burp. I actually had a teen in my youth group at another church who, while we were on a retreat, once recited the Lord's prayer while burping every word. One of the adult leaders was quite offended about this and asked the teen why he would defile the Lord's prayer in that way, and he said, "You know, I never really paid attention to the words of the Lord's prayer until I tried to burp every word. Do you know how hard that is?" He then gave us an impressive rendition of the Apostles' Creed.

And the fact is that not everyone has the spiritual gift of burping. And on the Day of Pentecost, all of the gifts are of the same Spirit. But most importantly, new language is being spoken.

*

When I teach an introduction to religion or an introduction to philosophy course at the local college, one of the most important things I do at the beginning of the course is to teach new vocabulary words, because you have to learn new words to learn philosophy and religion, and especially with philosophy, some words that we use in everyday life take on new meaning in philosophy. And the same is just like any job, you have special words for special things in the office or in the workplace that don't make much sense when you take them out of that context.

One helpful thing for us to do on this Pentecost is to think through words that are used only in churches or are used in special ways by the church. Here are a few that I came up with, just from looking at your bulletins and looking around the church: sanctuary, preludes, postludes, benedictions, doxologies, passing of the peace, hymnals, narthex, Lucifer, and stole. Or what about activities that we do?—consistory, communion, baptism. We can sing in church or outside of church, and we can eat together inside or outside of church. But eating and singing mean something different when we eat together at the Lord's Supper or at a church covered-dish.

Sometimes, too, we understand that the church and its vocabulary mean something hurtful to those outside of the church. Baptism and Communion, while we see them as activities that bring folks together, are often exclusionary practices, based on who has the privilege to receive baptism and communion whereas all others may not. I have been in churches in the midwest where women dare not speak in the sanctuary. In Catholic churches women may not read certain parts of the Bible aloud during the worship service.

The reality is that we live in a strange time when the lines between the church and the rest of the world have never been stranger, perhaps not as much since the very beginning of the church. Those outside of the church might look at our worship bulletin and say, "what in the world is an 'acolyte'?" Or someone might look at the church from the outside and remember a time when something abusive happened to them when they were an acolyte. I remember in the Methodist church my family joined when I was in middle school that they had strict rules about who could and couldn't be an acolyte, and I remember asking to do it one time and I was told no, because the cut-off was whatever grade I had just finished. It's not a big deal to me now, but I also remember this happening, and I remember the lady who said it to me. My memory of acolytes as a young teenager was being told "no." In like manner, for so many on the outside of the church, if they do speak the language, they know it as a foul language.

So on this Pentecost Sunday, on this day when we celebrate Communion and the rite of Confirmation for our Confirmands, we affirm together that we are reconciling as a church and moving toward Christianity becoming a Yes-saying religion, rather than one that is negative and is No-saying. As an affirmative faith, we as a congregation say to our confirmands, "yes!" We live in a world where so much of our culture is about saying "no," or that which appears to be something positive is very often a way in which our young people are commodified or exploited. We as a church want to work towards being a community where the gifts and talents of our young people are affirmed and explored, even when their gifts challenge us. In fact, in this community, we hope for and expect our young people to challenge us.

As an affirmative faith, we as a congregation celebrate the sacrament of communion openly, stating that this table is open for all who wish to partake. We may speak different languages and our words may conflict with each other, but the various faith languages which we bring to the table give us a fuller sense of the dis-membered Lord who is re-membered through the words of institution.

As an affirming faith, we openly celebrate Pentecost by praying that this church grows and reaches new people who look different from us and those who have different identities than our own. If we wanted to have a church where we simply cloned each other and wanted people all like ourselves, we should have just renovated our building to be a hall of mirrors. We affirm the different theological expressions latent within our little congregation, and hope that we do not cause division in the church and hope further that we become more diverse.

For some, Pentecost is the day when the One True Faith® was passed down to the faithful, 2,000 years ago. In fact, the narrow and angry religious discourses that dominate the radio and television in our country are a towering testament to this fact. However, *we* celebrate today that Pentecost is not a once and done event, but an ongoing one, that God—however we might define the divine—still speaks through the church and *through all of us*. And despite what we might interpret about our own experiences of church, whether it is being said "no" to in the past, or being told "yes" by being confirmed in this church today, or despite having an allergy or illiteracy to the church, for a church that believes in Pentecost, we must affirm that Pentecost is an ongoing event.

You know that there are Pentecostal Churches in our community. I propose that we are a *Pentecost-ing* church. A Pentecosting Church is one that perpetually celebrates Pentecost. Just as Jesus likened the coming of the Holy Spirit as being led to drink living waters, we affirm together that God is with us as a physical presence, as water in our bodies, but not just water in our bodies as a substance, but *living waters* in our bodies, animated by the air, the breath of the Spirit.

The Gospel of John says that the disciples of his time could not yet receive the Holy Spirit because Jesus was not yet glorified. But in an age where Christ has risen, and ascended, and the Spirit has become poured out upon us, we may now reverse this statement in the scripture. By living as one filled with living waters, we may now live so as to glorify the Lord.

This is now our challenge as we with humility seek to confirm by saying "yes" to our Confirmands and seek out a "yes" to ourselves by eating bread and drinking wine—together mixing to our bodies, made of living waters, water and the spirit with the gifts of the earth, so we may become for the world the body and blood of Christ.

You Put Your Weeds in There![1]

Matthew 13:24-30, 36-43 (Proper 11)

In just about everything, be it religion or politics, or even history, there's always an *us*, and then there's always a *them*. There's *we*, and then there's *they*. Children learn to differentiate *us* and *them* early. I remember watching *Sesame Street* as a child and having the blue Muppet, Grover, teach "near" and "far," teaching how to connect the use of pronouns with space, but there is always something different about "near" and "far" than "us" and "them": namely, the words or ideas of "us" and "them" aren't just about location as they are about categorizing people. And it's an unfortunate reality of human nature to do so from the beginning.

Jesus' parable of the seeds and the weeds is quite simple on a certain level, when we abuse its meaning: there's us, and then there's them. *We're* the good seed who grow into plants. Then there's the weeds, *them* weeds or *those* weeds. Weeds always sprout up, and when you go to harvest, if *they* survive, *they* get thrown to the fire. The fire is simply another word for Hell. So ignore the weeds, pull out the weeds, exterminate the weeds if you have to. The weeds will always be there, but there's a flaming destination to the weeds no matter how much they prosper. They can grow tall and they can have beautiful flowers, but they're still weeds, and they're all destined for Hell. The fact is that so much of human history is based upon this basic metaphor: *us vs. them*, the good crop and the weeds.

But when it comes to the idea of "hell," which Jesus is invoking here, it's very easy to look at those who are "not us" and say, well, that's who Jesus is talking about: *those who are "not us."* It's also very easy to look at difficult times we might have in our lives, and conclude that our bad times are upon us because

God is punishing us, throwing us out to burn with the weeds. But do we really believe in this idea of Hell?

Recently the idea of "universalism," or *universal salvation*, the idea that there is no hell, has become controversial among Christian circles; a pastor named Rob Bell recently published a book titled *Love Wins*, where he questions whether hell is a real place or not. So controversial has this book become that his other books have been banned by other pastors and he has been declared a heretic by many churches.[2] In North Carolina, and this is a true story, a young pastor sent a Facebook message out to his friends, including his parishioners, that he was just reading this book, *Love Wins*, and when he came to church the following Sunday, he was informed by his church board that after meeting with his Bishop without his knowledge during the week, he was being fired. A pastor was terminated from his job for openly admitting that he had read the book. That pastor is now without a church and without work.[3]

The question is, if there is no hell, what's the point of going to church? What's the point in being "good" for Jesus if there is no hell? I think that these questions are really about asking how there can be an us-versus-them view of the world if there is no hell. What will happen to "those people" or "them," if "we" are all saved? As you probably know the Lutheran church is currently involved in a small schism—it's now public knowledge that the Lutheran church around the corner from us has left their denomination—and Lutheranism in America likes to split and break away from other churches, it's just part of their history. When I was in Divinity School I took some language classes at the Lutheran Seminary nearby, and the students there used to have a joke about how there needed to be many rooms in heaven for the different branches of the Lutheran church, because if the Missouri Synod or Wisconsin Synod Lutherans showed up to heaven and saw anyone but them there they would be convinced they were in hell!

For me, the idea of hell does not have to be about God necessarily dividing the good crop and the weeds, but it forces us to think, in Jesus' terms, about ourselves like a garden. There are some vegetables we don't like; for me, I don't like eggplant. If I came to a patch of eggplants, I would walk away, no matter how good the eggplants are. What is considered a good crop and what gets thrown to the fire as a weed is largely subjective, and is based on what *we* contribute to those around us, the passersby to the garden.

For many, the belief in hell puts a big fence around the garden of God, clearly defining "us" and "them." But the fence designating what is hell and what is not is something those inside of the garden get to dictate. But the fact is that Hell is a matter of perspective; those on the outside might look in and see that the belief in hell isn't something that sets "us" free from the inside, but rather, it makes the fire *surround* us in a way that we have no escape from the prison that our own beliefs construct. *Hell, then, it would seem, isn't really then the habitat of those outside of "our" church or our own ideology* as much as *our construction of hell is the entrapment of ourselves.*

A better way to think about hell, which subverts the us-versus-them mentality, turns the cameras upon ourselves to realize the hell we create for ourselves and others. To believe in the resurrected Christ, to believe that ours is a true religion, is *not* license to give everyone else Hell but to understand that we ourselves are now playing with fire, and we can be responsible or irresponsible with that fire. We can use the fire to change the world, and mould it into something new, or we can use the fire to burn others and ourselves. We have seen how much of Christian history has been wrapped up in the burning of witches, or the burning of heretics, or the burning of books. It is now time for us to use the fire of Christ not to burn the rest of the world at the stake but to create something new, and transfigure and cook up a new world.

To do this requires us to turn the heat on ourselves, and acknowledge that we don't always know the answers to all of the questions. But we can find a graceful walk where we journey together and work to make the world a better place even if we can't find absolute agreement with each other. In this version of the faith, hell is not necessarily the threat of annihilation by fire or eternal punishment in the lake of fire, but is the challenge and wager handed to us by Jesus: will we give the world hell, or will we give the world hope?

Slapped by Your Grandma!

Matthew 14:22-23 (Proper 14)

An Irish boy had heard stories of his father, and his grandfather, and his father before, that on their eighteenth birthdays they walked *across* the lake from their homestead to the village to get their first drink at the old pub on the other side of the lake. This was part of the legend that nothing will stand in the way of a man in his family and his drink.

So the boy waited until the hot summer day of his eighteenth birthday, and he assumed that it was now his turn to continue the legend of his father, and his grandfather, and his father before that. He went out onto the dock, stepping out onto the water, and immediately fell in.

Walking back, soaking wet, he went to his grandmother's to tell her that he could not walk across the lake like his father, and his grandfather, and his father before that. He said, I've been a good Irish boy: I love my mother; I pray to Our Lady the Holy Virgin; and I don't like Protestants. Why am I not as holy as my ancestors? The grandmother slapped him and said, you're not as smart as they were!

The boy was even more ashamed, and a little angry. He asked, crying, "why am I not as smart as my ancestors?"

The grandma said, your father, and your grandfather, and his father before that, were all born in January! This is August!

*

So often the story of Jesus walking on water is a story about faith—it's a miracle story that you either believe, or you don't. But I suggest this morning that we move beyond that question and search into what the story might mean if we ask some good questions.

The symbol of water in this story is important, and at different times and in different contexts in the Bible the symbol of water means something very different. Sometimes water is a symbol of the pagan gods—the rival god named in the Old Testament as a rival to the God of the Jews, Dagon, was the God of the seas. So whenever there is imagery of God hitting or slapping the seas in the Hebrew scriptures, it would have been read by the Jews as God showing dominance over Dagon, who was the God whose idol was trampled by the presence of the Ark of the Covenant in 1 Samuel.

Some scholars also note that in Genesis, the symbol of water is a symbol for the Mesopotamian goddess Ti'amet, a sea monster who is the goddess of the feminine and the uncontrollable chaos of the strong seas—it is no mistake that the rage of the ocean was equated with the fury of a woman searching for revenge.

This symbol of water is the "deep" which God sweeps over, divides and places a dome as a firmament, to separate the waters at the beginning of creation.[1] Moses, we remember, divided the sea to lead his people to slavery. Before that the world was flooded, and only a few humans and some animals were spared by the flood on Noah's ark. Droplets of water were placed in the sky and are the elemental requirements for the rainbow, hung in the sky as a symbol of God's promises to his people. And, of course, Jesus' ministry begins with the act of being baptized by John in the Jordan River.

Now here we have Jesus walking on water. A question to ask, then, is one of mechanics: *how* might we imagine this happening as this story would have been heard by a first-century audience?

One time one of my students who was an atheist and thought anyone who had any religion was just stupid, said to me that Christians don't know enough about their own religion to know that Jesus couldn't have walked on water. I asked him to explain this, expecting him to give me the line about science disproving religion, but instead he said that "everyone knows that Jesus had holes in his feet, so he surely would have just sunk." (Except that he forgot that the walking on water bit happened before Jesus' death.)

But I wonder: Did Jesus' feet get wet? In other words, did the water push up on Jesus, as if he was controlling the waters, as if the dome that God placed at the beginning of creation to control the waters *pushed up* onto the soles of Jesus' feet to support his weight? If this is how it happened, then the scripture is recalling water as the symbol of creation, reminding us that Jesus is the first-begotten, the first born of all of the universe, and that all of the world has been waiting this moment for Jesus to come and show himself.

Or if Jesus' feet didn't get wet, as in he glided just above the water, I imagine him walking like a child does on a big bank of snow, where the child isn't heavy enough to break the top of the snow. Here, it would seem that we are reminded again of creation, of God sweeping over the face of the deep, creating a new faith in those who witnessed the event.

Or if Jesus remains above the waters, could this be a symbol of baptism? These past few weeks I've been reading a book by the French philosopher René Girard called *Things Hidden Since the Foundation of the World*.[2] In the book, the philosopher analyzes all religious ritual from the perspective of violence, that all rituals either enact or mask violence of some sort.

I was baptized as a baby in a church, and most of us here were probably baptized by having water sprinkled on our heads. In many churches as you know, baptism must be done in a tank or in a river and you have to get dunked. People who insisted that there is a difference between the two didn't make much sense to me before—*why would this matter?* But what I am getting out of this book, and I am changing my mind about this, is that there is a difference in the ways we get baptized. Baptism is a ritual which re-enacts a drowning. You are drowned and then you are raised. And when you are raised, you are "born again." Your old self dies when you go down into the water and your new self is actualized in the moment you breathe upon coming out, like a child breathing her first breath upon entrance to a new world. And it's true that those of us who like baptizing without the dunking allow this element—this element of *violence*—of the ritual to be forgotten.

So in our story, the disciples see Jesus, who is believed to be a ghost, levitating above the water in the storm, and Peter thinking it's some kind of trick, asks Jesus to command him to come out to the water, and Jesus agrees, ordering him to come into the water—we might even ask whether it was ethical of Jesus to tell Peter to come out into the water, knowing that he would sink! And Jesus saves Peter when he sinks, and has an I-told-you-so moment, asking him, "You of little faith, why did you doubt?" It was Peter who clearly had enough faith to step out into the water, so what little faith is Jesus talking about?

It is almost as if Jesus, standing above the water, re-enacts a baptism here with the actual threat of death, of violence in the water. The lack of faith here is a lack of faith in the seriousness of the moment, and not a lack of faith in Jesus. Peter might have had too much faith in himself and not enough faith in the reality that the storm around him threatened much danger.

So for many of us this story teaches us that we should either stay safe on the boat, and let Jesus flout "out there" enough that he is some kind of "Holy Ghost" who we dare to call us into danger. For some of us this story is about stepping out into danger, and to accept the authority of what we think Jesus is telling us at any given time.

But here is where our baptism and our call to being born anew, to understand just how fragile our lives are, and to recognize the storm happening around us *slaps* us in the face, no matter what Holy Ghosts we think we see in the distance or how many times we jump off into the water.

*

I've been following in the news the last two weeks about a church in Middletown, Pennsylvania, that is in such turmoil with the calling of a new pastor that police have been called to make sure the worship service goes as planned, and a video was posted on the internet of people in the church yelling at the pastor in the middle of the sermon, saying, among other things, that Satan sent the pastor there.[3]

The fact is this is a church that has gone through five pastors in eight years and apparently has had nearly as many Christian Education directors and custodians in the same amount of time. The church has a huge children's program for neighborhood kids on Wednesdays, but they can't agree on the direction of the church to the point that a small group of people are now worshiping separately from the other church on Sundays, as of last week.

The heartbreaking thing when you see the video of people yelling at the pastor is that the church is nearly empty. The people are fighting over a building of empty pews. Clearly, this is a church that has lost its mission. They're certainly willing to be bold and take risks, even leaving their building behind them, but they have clearly lost touch with their community. But the risks they're really willing to take are very dangerous, and perhaps even destructive. Their church members are calling the local radio stations saying that communists have taken over their church—this kind of rhetoric hasn't worked since McCarthy was accusing people of being Red. This is how stuck in the past this church is.

Jesus is calling us *not* to just step out into the storm in faith, and Jesus is calling us not only to recognize his presence in the winds and turmoil of the storm—but there's more. Jesus is challenging us to *take the storm seriously*, to understand that what we do in church can burn us badly, and it can burn us out, if we're not careful. And when we're getting burned we're no longer attracting newcomers or our children to the faith.

We need to take seriously that the Gospel is powerful, and if we're not careful we can drown in something that is meant to save us. We need to allow the storm to slap us in the face once in a while for a reality check. Living out our baptisms in a serious way is this challenge to which we as a church are called.

The 9-12 Error!

Genesis 11:1-9; Exodus 14:19-31 (Proper 19)

This sermon was preached on the tenth anniversary of the September 11, 2001, terror attacks on the United States, on September 11, 2011.

It's been ten years since September 11th, 2001, as you've surely been hearing from radio, television, and every other media outlet for the past two weeks. September 11th also holds significance to me because it was the day I was baptized as an infant in 1977, before I was quite six months old. I was obviously too young to remember my own baptism but it was on this date, September 11, 1977, that I began my formal life in the church, baptized in a country church, an Evangelical Congregational Church, outside of the town of Columbia, Pennsylvania.

On the twenty-fourth anniversary of my baptism, in 2001, I was working as a campus minister at DePaul University, and since it was a Tuesday morning, my ministry team members always had a very early-morning breakfast meeting. While the meeting was going on, we usually had *The Today Show* on the television, and as a result we happened to watch the events of the day progress on live television, while most of the campus of DePaul University was still asleep. Around the city of Chicago, rumors began about plans to take down the skyscrapers in Chicago. The city's public transportation system was shut down. More rumors began about someone assaulting a Muslim not too far off of campus in retaliation. We were concerned about the safety of the students on the campus, and some of our concern was to distract ourselves from the news and rumors of news happening all around us.

So much was going on that day, trying to keep freshman students, who had just moved to the city for their first weeks of college, from moving into a state of hysteria, that I wouldn't realize until days later, as mentioned before, I had actually planned on going to the Chicago Cubs vs. Saint Louis Cardinals game on that afternoon—everything inessential seemed to stop and change. That evening, my supervisor and friend, Javier, and I had a bite to eat together and we began to decompress everything that had happened for the day. We concluded that September 11 was going to begin a new era of the ugliness of religion to emerge in new forms.

And I think we were right. Before the fires of Ground Zero were even extinguished, Jerry Falwell and Pat Robertson began to preach that the events of September 11 indicated that God was punishing our country for doing something wrong. In an interview just days after September 11, Jerry Falwell said that the reason why God allowed us to be attacked was because the feminists, the gays, pro-choice politicians, and the ACLU were being given too much voice in our country, and Robertson agreed. After a public outcry for these statements, as you probably know, both of them apologized. But we know that they really meant what they said.

What is interesting to me is that if one is to believe such thinking, that God punished us on September 11th by commanding Muslims to conspire against us, one must then assume that this supposedly Christian God is using very specific forms of Islam to do 'His' work. And furthermore, we should not forget that this is exactly the theological position of the Westboro Baptist Church, which protests soldiers' funerals with picket signs that say "Thank God for September 11."

When the towers fell, when we realized that the Pentagon had been attacked, and when the rumors were confirmed that another airplane had crashed in Pennsylvania, we were quick to assume that the Pillar of Cloud that had been protecting America from collapse for 200 years had suddenly been lifted, and that the judgment of our nation was about to emerge. *Our* mistake was to assume that the Pillar of Cloud was protecting us in the first place *simply* because we are Americans. And instead of really thinking through what had just happened, we as a nation were quick to point fingers and use the events as an excuse to go to war. Instead of rising above the terror and the terrorists, we declared a war on terror and defined it as a roundabout way of seeking revenge, almost believing that if we sought out vengeance our God would bring his smile back upon our nation.

On September 11, ten years ago today, 3,000 Americans were killed in a horrible act of terror. Beginning September 12, we have seen just under 6,000 American servicemen killed, 42,700 American military wounded. If we count American civilians, since September 12, 2001, we have seen just under 52,000 American casualties. In Iraq, over a million more have died, mostly civilians, though we don't really know the numbers. In Afghanistan, between 4,000 and 5,000 more people have died; in Pakistan we have killed around 2,000 more; in Somalia we only have data for one year, 2007, and the death toll was around 7,000. And we continue to pay to continue this war on terror; by the end of this year the estimated spending to fund all of this killing is about $1.283 trillion, or about 11 percent of our total national debt.

For me, September 11 has become a day of the tragedy of religion; what religions cause us to do and what fuels us to continue the cycle of violence. Some of the national rhetoric today is to glorify September 12, the day after September 11th, as a day we came together as a nation. The error or mistake of September 12 was believing that we needed to act in such a way to gain back the pillar of cloud that we had lost, and that if we could only gain back the favor of God we would once again be the great nation we once were or were once meant to be by throwing the rest of the world into the Red Sea. Our pretentiousness is instead to rebuild the tower of Babel in the world by enacting war wherever air is breathed.

The error of September 12 was to trust in ourselves and to once again declare that America is the "Hope of the World" when we know it is not, and we all know that it is a lie. If we are a Baptized People and we pledge absolute authority to our nation, *to the point of slaughtering over a million people in Iraq in the last ten years*, we are not only lying to ourselves about our Baptism *but we have betrayed the very essence of Christianity* that our parents, and our grandparents, and their grandparents have handed down to us in the font of our faith. If we are to continue the cycle of violence and if we remain silent about the reality of violence which we are *both* apathetic to, *and* participating in by our silence, we worship the very Satan which we point to the rest of the world as having worshiped, believing that everyone else is the Devil. We even go so far as to call them the "axis of evil": in doing so, we prove just how quickly we forget our own sin and how quickly we cast the first stone.

It is now time for us, now that ten years have passed, to begin to be honest about the horror that we have brought to this world as a nation beginning September 12, 2001. We have multiplied the deaths of those who died on September 11 many times over. We have proven to the world just how deep our obsession for revenge runs. We have proven to ourselves that the monster of terrorism is more often among ourselves than everywhere else. This cycle of violence, this ongoing crucifixion of the world, can only finally find an end with the peace which comes from Christ, yet instead of preaching hope and courage we have given the world Hell.

As we memorialize with nostalgia those who have died on this day, we must remember the millions more whose deaths were *prefigured by our refusal* to ask tough questions, to seek answers, and work towards reconciliation. Jesus, and the healing of genuine forgiveness, is not the *answer* to our question, but rather our discipleship to Jesus is the answer to *the question* which lingers while we so easily remember the dead without asking the big questions which this date now symbolizes.

For me, September 11 is a day of tragedy, not in spite of the coincidence that it is the day of my baptism. It is a tragedy *because* the past ten years are witness to the failure of our supposedly Christian nation to remember our baptisms, which have either been drown out in our need to perpetuate violence or seem to be an excuse for us to continue the cycle of violence.

We now must ask: Before we take this date seriously, how many more millions have to die? Do we continue to support and look the other way to all of the violence *because* of our baptism, and why has our shared baptism not caused us to question our violent response to violence? Will we undo the error of terror of September 12 on *this* September 11?

Do You Want Steak or Salad?

Genesis 4:1-16; Philippians 2:1-13; Psalm 25:1-9 (Proper 21)

The story of Cain and Abel is one we can probably all relate to—those of us who have brothers or sisters know that at different times in our lives we are rivals to the other, or at least we sometimes believe that we are rivals to the other. Siblings always think that they are less favorable to their parents than the other, and in some cases I think parents encourage sibling rivalry, whether they know it or not.

And sibling rivalry isn't something that just goes away over time, or it doesn't really disappear as we get older, it takes on different forms. I am sure you have experienced a funeral where siblings wouldn't sit anywhere near each other or someone felt slighted over the other in the way in which an estate is divided. In fact, I was recently asked to help mediate a situation in the community for individuals (not at all affiliated with the church), where the three children of a deceased parent are suing each other; the parent had different wills that were filed with different lawyers, and then suddenly a fourth sibling has emerged that no one had seen for decades and he has provided documentation that makes a claim to the estate. The reality is that one of the siblings is now very wealthy, where the others are not, and he is intentionally pushing the legal issues without compromise so that there will be nothing left to split up when it's all over because of the legal fees involved. I am sure we all have stories that are like this in some way.

Recently I've been reading some books by René Girard on the history of violence in religion, and one place we must all start if we are to think about this issue is Cain's murder of his brother, Abel. It's the first murder in the Bible, and Abel is the first martyr.

What's interesting about this story, if you take a couple steps back from it, is that Cain, who is a farmer, gets jealous of Abel, a shepherd, because Cain feels that God delights more in Abel's blood offerings of animals to God than in Cain's offerings of grain. In fact, it wasn't just Cain that felt that way; the Bible clearly states that God showed favoritism toward Abel's offerings.

When Cain spoke to God about it, God more or less showed ambivalence, and instead of being completely honest with Cain, he spoke in a kind of foreshadowing riddle, downplaying Cain's anger and saying that if he does not master his sin, it will overtake him, as the sin is "crouching at the door." We should be mindful here of the way the Bible tells the story; it is clear that God showed favoritism toward Abel and that God did not really show Cain a way to truly overcome this resentment other than side-stepping Cain's anger. And it could be that Cain's anger was so deep that God knew what was about to happen, or that the evil inherent in human beings was inevitably going to emerge between the first two siblings.[1]

The professions of the brothers has a lot to do with what is happening in the story. Cain was a farmer who gave grain offerings and Abel was a shepherd who gave blood offerings, and it's clear that God favored the blood offerings. As humans eat meat products and plants, both shepherds and farmers are necessary, but giving up your steak is a bit different than giving up your salad for God.

One of the theories about this story is that all human beings have a lust for blood. If you really want a steak, is any amount of salad going to satisfy you? If I really want a burger, if you give me a pepper and say "eat," I am still going to want the burger. For the majority of us who eat meat, you know there is nothing like a juicy steak. We want to taste the blood, and nothing quite satisfies our hunger for meat other than meat. If you are a *real* carnivore, you're not going to be tricked by a veggie-burger most of the time. It's just not the same. And, it would seem from scripture, we are created in God's image, and God clearly prefers the offerings of the animals than the fruits and grains.

So the theory is that Cain's immediate turn to kill his brother is about getting God's favor, but it is also about the fact that Cain had a very base, very human need to kill and to spill blood. Abel had animals to give as a sacrifice, and Cain showed God how much he wanted God to be pleased with him by offering a human sacrifice of his own brother. It's worth noting that while God punished Cain, Cain got to survive and was granted a mark of safety by God. And Cain got to be primary ancestor of much of humanity. The Bible didn't say this, but there is a tradition of interpreting this passage of scripture which suggests that Cain may have had exclusive reproductive rights over his other sisters now that Abel was eliminated as sexual competition, although the Bible only identifies one of Cain's sisters as his wife.

The point is that Cain got to survive and because he killed Abel, he won the sibling rivalry between himself and his brother, whether he won it in a good way or not. But this is the beginning of the history of violence that proceeds from this point in the Bible, and the descendants of Cain were so bad, minus Noah, that God had to get rid of all of them at one point. It would seem, then, that the whole history of the world is a footnote to Cain killing Abel, that all of the violence in the world, whether it's between boys fighting in a playground or countries dropping bombs on other countries, is an extension of an argument about women or an argument about who is more favored by God, or whose God favors which nation more. Again, the history of the world can be summarized into one short story in the fourth chapter of Genesis.

Except for one thing—and this is the only exception. The sacrifice of Christ on the cross, the sacrifice of God dying for our sins, is the event of history which interrupts this cycle of violence. Our reading from Saint Paul, in his letter to the Philippians, is one of the perennial examples of how Christ is a reversal of the downward cycle of the world. Scholars believe that this poem may have been an early song that was sung for a baptism. God, the scriptures tell us, "emptied himself, taking on the form of a human slave"—what was outside of space and time has now entered space and time. What is regal and kingly has now been made manifest in poverty, on the margins of society. What was pure spirit is now part of human flesh. What could not die is now known best to us by a death—the worst death humanly imaginable on a cross.

In other words, the cycle of violence of human beings, instigated by a human sinful need to offer blood sacrifice to prove one's good standing with God, has now been interrupted, negated, and absolved by God's own sacrifice of himself on the cross. As an act of love, God loves his people that he gave as a human sacrifice his only-begotten son, that whosoever believes in him should not perish but have everlasting life. The self-sacrifice of Jesus calls us and challenges us to first believe in God's sacrifice, but in response we must sacrifice our own need to kill, and to backbite, and to create a ruckus, and to exert our superiority over others.

This is to say that Christ is the answer to the problem of human violence, but it is an answer that we as a society, and we as a nation, and we as a human race, have over and over again refused to accept, even while we say we accept it. We accept Jesus yet we want to still wage war. We say that we profess Christ, yet we want to limit the rights of others in our allegedly Christian nation. We say that Christ is the greatest story ever told, and the more we try to believe in it literally, the *less* we really take seriously God's conclusion to the story, that the violence of the world ends in God's own radically violent act of sacrificing himself through a blood sacrifice on the cross.

We love to say we have some personal relationship with Jesus yet we don't really accept the true challenge to the world offered to us in Christ, that Christ alone offers us a narrow passage out of the endless cycle of violence that begins with Abel's blood being swallowed up by the ground just east of the Garden of Eden. Instead, when we are reminded of the world-changing power of Jesus, we look to God and say, like Cain, "It wasn't my turn to watch Abel," even while the blood of the world and the blood of God himself are dripping out of our hands and out of our pockets.

When I worked as a youth minister I often wondered what the point of religious education is. Many of us have been deeply influenced by the Sunday School movement, and many churches are now saying that the Sunday School is an idea no longer worth pursuing. In this church we have many dedicated volunteers to our children's religious education and it is important that we teach the next generation the faith entrusted to us. And we should celebrate this commitment that is made through the hard work of volunteers and your money that you put in the plate that supports our children and youth programs.

But we adults need to ask ourselves, especially in this late summer and early autumn when children return to schools and families return to church after a summer hiatus: Is the Christianity we are passing down to our children one that we really believe to have the power to change lives and to change the world, *or* do we just like the way it sounds when we say those words? Do we educate the children so they will conform to the authority of their parents and the church to keep the institution of the church really going forward, *or* do we want to raise up young Christians who want to be sent out from this church to challenge the status quo (rather than just continue the status quo), and to show the world a better way through Christ? Do we really want to let our faith, especially the faith of our children, to light the world on fire, or to keep it contained to the couple candles we let them light in church on Sundays?

These are our challenges today as we open our Sunday School year, and as we baptize someone new in our community, and every time we celebrate communion or observe the Sabbath: our prayer must be for a *reversal* of this world—a *reversal* whose power *can* happen in our church classrooms or through our font. We just have to ask whether we really believe in what we say that we believe.

Worshiping the Golden Calf

Exodus 32:1-15 (Proper 23)

Our Bible reading from Exodus is one of the events leading up to Moses returning from the top of the mountain with the tablets containing the Ten Commandments; this is a story that is vivid in many of our imaginations. I don't remember what age it was that I saw the classic film, *The Ten Commandments*, with Charlton Heston, but whenever I hear these stories from scripture I think of the same scene from the movie. The Israelites get tired of waiting for Moses, and after all that they have been through, after all the times that God had pulled strings for them and saved them, they just got bored waiting for Moses to come down from the mountain and constructed a new God to worship!

On one hand, this story really dumbfounds me. The movie version, if you remember, really played up the emphasis of the creation of the new idol to worship. The Israelites just need to worship *something*, they just need to worship *anything*, and they melt their gold together to create a golden calf. And when they created this new idol the ecstasy that was just brimming under the surface of their anxious wait for Moses finally erupted, to the point that the women were rubbing their hair on the golden idol. It was not just a spiritual need that was being fulfilled by the idol but also a physical need to worship something they could physically see. They were tired of this other God; even though he did great things he occasionally disappeared and did not give them exactly what they wanted in the moment that they always wanted it.

They needed something they could touch, something to pray at, and something they could physically locate. Something that could be lifted, carried around, and put on parade. Their God who had stuck with them, on the other hand, was an air God, usually invisible and presented his presence in bizarre and unexpected ways. The good thing about the air God is that the God of air could be anywhere, but air doesn't really ever become solid. It's hard to parade around a God of air. Their God's *weakness* to the Israelites waiting for Moses is that Yahweh is *invisible* and *difficult to grasp*. We know today that air is a substance made up of different gasses and atoms. But back then air was metaphysically understood by most cultures to be a *nothing*. This is why it is so philosophically radical in the Bible that God breathes life into Adam; life is *blown* through the wind that gives the living breath. Other cultures understood life to be indicative of blood, for example, but for Judaism life is in the air. Other gods around them were gods of the lands, or of the waters, so the idea of a God of air for whom no idols can possibly be made was probably a joke to those in other cultures around them. It's telling that while this idolatry was going on, God made a clear commandment against idolatry.

So the Israelites got tired of waiting for this air God and constructed a new god to take its place: a golden calf, made of the finest metals and jewels, a God of *lavish abundance*, quite literally acting as a *substitution* for the God of air.

Even though this idea of worshiping a golden calf might seem like a foreign, arcane, and ancient idea, the reality is that the worship of false gods continues today. We have people running for political office, for example, who think their ideas are going to save the world; and I am sure you know people, or hear them on the radio, who believe that their political knowledge is elevated; that it nearly eclipses God. As some say when talking politics, "Talent on loan from God." *This* is idolatry, often veiled as an act of humility ("on loan"), and when it is employed by politicians and demagogues—especially when the discourse follows that possessions and so-called "civil rights" are placed above human lives—this idolatry is particularly dangerous.

We also know folks for whom their religion becomes idolatry.

I have met too many pastors in my short career who have not only elevated their experience and themselves above just about everyone else around them, but then they use their own sense of privilege to make others worship their authority, often in indirect and esoteric ways. Or people not in the religion business who create a kind of religious system in their workplaces or in their families that generate a new way of worshiping the one with power. Idolatry is seemingly everywhere, and idolatry is always re-inventing itself to take on new forms.

The radical theologian Gabriel Vahanian has written that even our basic ideas about God betray us and make us idolaters when we are not careful. Many of us have the image of the long-bearded white guy who lives "up there" as God—I call this image the "cosmic Santa Claus"—and we know how and why this image is wrong, and even dangerous when taken literally. Yet we all hold on to it, and we all know how the Christian God becomes a kind of divine Santa Claus in popular Christianity and in the Gospel of Wealth.[1]

The theologian Vahanian goes even further, though, saying that even the word "God" becomes an idolatry.[2] What he means by this is that if one looks at the way in which the word "God" is used in our culture, the word "God" is probably invoked more in swearing and in pornography than we'd probably like to admit. For example, what does it really mean when we sing "God Bless America" at a baseball game? Or when we proclaim "In God we trust" on our coins? What does it mean, beyond a political defin-ition, when we pledge allegiance to a flag that represents "one nation under God?" We know that God does not care whether we invoke his name in the pledge of allegiance. We know, if we are honest, that God does not favor our nation over others just because we are who we are or because we invoke the word "God" in our pledge *to a flag*.

In fact, if one takes our language seriously, invoking God while *pledging allegiance to a flag* is taking the name of God in vain.

It is blasphemous; if we are not careful about what it really is we are saying and which objects we *pledge our allegiances to.* This is obvious, though I know that this is also controversial: our allegiances to the divine must be radically different, and radically more demanding than anything we should expect to offer to our country. Clearly, to relegate God to statements and pledges, and patriotic statements, and empty words sung at sports events, or on our money, *we commit idolatry.* Vahanian and other radical theologians (Hamilton, in particular) have suggested that we attempt to not use the word "God" because of the real danger, the real idolatry we strike up when we use the word improperly.[3]

When we take a look at ourselves and our religious actions and our language seriously, we are probably surprised at the false Gods that we create. We don't even need to look that far to find our golden calves; we too often bring them with us to church. They are quite obviously seen in the record section of our checkbooks. Which golden calves are present to us in this church? Which golden calves am I leading you towards in my preaching? Where are the golden calves in our homes, and computers, and which ideas or ideologies do we idolize falsely? And for what purposes do we use the word "God?" As we ourselves wait and long to hear the voice and image of God, and grow weary of prayers not answered *exactly* the way we want them to be, we must ask: we're not so different, are we?

Circumcisions, Cheap!

Romans 2:17-29; Matthew 23:1-12
(Proper 26/Reformation Sunday)

Recently I had a conversation with a laywoman who was going through one of those self-guided one-year Bibles with her husband, which is a way that one reads through the whole Bible in one year. Most people give up when they get to Leviticus, because that can be pretty boring, but they got through it.

The woman asked me if I could explain something to them. She said that her husband was too embarrassed to ask me about this, and suddenly I became even more curious regarding what she wanted to ask.

While reading the Torah, the necessity of circumcision as a man of faith became clear, and not being circumcised, he wanted to know whether he should consider being circumcised.

My first response was that *no*, he should not feel compelled to be circumcised for his faith, unless he's really into that sort of thing. And furthermore: I didn't take the circumcision class in divinity school, so he would have to talk to a doctor about all of that.

In all seriousness, this is a very good question.

Jews perform circumcisions as a means of marking their boys as an outward sign of God's covenant with his people. There have been times in history where circumcision has become problematic, such as during the Holocaust, when Jewish boys would be identified as Jewish when picked up off of the streets, based on their circumcisions. In this sense, the idea of a boy being circumcised was not only a mark of covenant but a mark of death. Being counted as one of God's own, and being marked in a way that could identify you when you are being persecuted—and we should remember that Jews have been persecuted in most parts of the world throughout history—is, to make a bad pun, a double-edged knife.

The question arose in the early days of the Christian church about circumcision, a controversy about whether Christian men and boys had to be circumcised. This is the exact same question of the couple reading through the Torah. Paul says pretty much the same thing that Jesus said in our reading this morning, that circumcision or anything else in the law has no meaning if it is not meaningful to you. Circumcision is a mark on your flesh and, Paul says, only has meaning if the code of the law, or the covenant with God is interior, or inside of you. Otherwise it is something only outward, and I think we should not obscure that when Paul talks about circumcision he is talking about a mark on the sexual organ, which is traditionally seen as a site of sin, even though when we think about the idea of circumcision we forget this fact. In other words, do men really act differently because they have a mark committing them to God on their sexual organs, or do men just forget about this? Or does the language of "covenant" and "law" not seem to have anything to do with what we do with, or to, our bodies?

So for St. Paul, he says, if you have been circumcised, your circumcision is an oath or a covenant that your flesh has with God and you must continue to follow the law, but you should understand that accepting Christ as your Lord and savior completes the law, even as Jesus liberates you from the law. In other words, what you will be ultimately judged for is your allegiance to Jesus, but your circumcision still binds you to your race.

One way this idea has played out in Christian history is the idea that you can incorporate your ethnic identity or your racial background into your Christian practice. We should remember the majority of Christians, once the religion took off outside of Jewish territories, were formerly pagans from a variety of religions, including the ancient Greek, Roman, Egyptian, and

Mesopotamian paganisms, the Persian religion of Zoroastrianism, and later the indigenous religions of Germany and England. Today we might think of Christianity as a closed system in many ways, but one of the reasons why Christianity spread so quickly was because you could mix in your former religious background into Christianity so long as you accepted the Good News of Jesus Christ, broadly defined, and placed your ethnicity, your racial identity, and even your nationality as secondary to your Christianity.

This is why, for example, Catholicism is called the "Catholic" church, namely, because "catholic" means universal. And this is why, for example, Easter and Christmas are still celebrated on dates that used to be ancient pagan holidays. Or why we generally tolerate, or even celebrate, the practice of bringing a tree into our home during the winter. This practice was once done by pagan Germans to honor the gods of life, as represented by the tree, and welcoming the tree into your home as a guest during the coldest time of the year. So long as these practices didn't contradict the Gospel, you could continue to celebrate or observe these traditions. In many cases, the practices continued but simply took on new meanings within the religion of Christianity.

Sometimes I teach this history of Christianity to folks and they don't believe it, because Christianity is supposed to be a strict religion. In fact, depending who you ask, many people see Christianity as this tremendously closed and conservative system of beliefs, and they are afraid of the church because we as the church represent the face of this closed, strict system of beliefs. Christians, it would seem in America, are supposed to be upper-class, vote a certain way, and dress a certain way, and if you have done certain things in your past, you have a lot to confess and be sorry for before you may begin to participate in the life of the church.

Yet for others, Christianity is a religion that has become too liberal. You all know I love to listen to the preacher from

Philadelphia that comes on the local radio at noon on Sundays, it is a broadcast of the World Wide Truth of God Church with Pastor Gino Jennings. Most of his sermons are about other churches, namely us, who require your pastor to go to school, and not only allow women to speak in church but to be pastors, and sometimes even allows gays, or even worse, divorced men and women to speak and be ministers in the church. For these folks, there is some sense that Jesus established a very clear-cut religion that does not have any shades of gray about it, and that of course, their local interpretation of Christianity is not *the* only kind of true Christianity possible, but it is the only *possible* kind of Christianity possible.

So, here we stand on this final Sunday of October, which is always remembered as Reformation Sunday, where we remember how right we Protestants were when we stood with Martin Luther as he nailed his 95 theses on the church door in Wittenberg, Germany, which began the process of the Catholic church losing religious, political, scientific, and economic control over much of Europe. But we have seen that Protestantism has turned into something far worse than Martin Luther believed Catholicism was or would become. The Catholic church believed, during the Reformation, if individual Christians had too much say in the beliefs of the church, we would start getting some strange ideas going around. And, no matter which side you sit on in the debate about whether Christianity is too liberal or too conservative today, you probably agree that there are some strange religious ideas out there, and often they occur in the church.

*

Those of you who are on Facebook know that I've been having a kind of public conversation with one of my friends, who still goes to the church where I grew up. He said that last Sunday the new pastor announced that they were having a 10-week sermon series on stewardship that was to begin last Sunday. Now this is not all that unusual there, because I am pretty sure they had a two-year series on stewardship a few years ago, or at least it seemed that it went on that long! Now, my friend doesn't have a problem with talking about money in church, it is necessary, but he said that the week before this the preacher just finished preaching a sermon about our subject today, the circumcision of the heart, Romans 2, about how Christianity no longer binds us to the law of the Jews.

My friend asked the pastor why it is that we are allowed to eat pork or shrimp, and the pastor said, "that's a great example of how laws of Judaism no longer apply to us." So then my friend asked, why it is that their church does not allow homosexuality, since the law against that is in the same verse in Leviticus. Now my friend did not say this in a mocking way, because he is actually someone who believes that gays should not be allowed to be in leadership positions in the church.

But the Pastor's response was unsatisfying: simply, "this is what the rules are in our denomination."

You see, sometimes we say we are liberated from one set of rules, only to repeat those rules in a new set of rules. This is not what Jesus or Paul had in mind at all, and this is precisely why Paul wrote what he did to the church in Rome which was having a controversy about circumcision. Paul said that circumcision isn't what saves you, even though it may be an important or valid spiritual practice or identity, but the process of circumcising your heart is what molds you into a place of sanctification and holiness. Just saying that you're saved, or yelling "Amen," or putting money in the plate doesn't save you, but these practices might be outward signs of your inner circumcision. But they could be to put on a big show, too, and God knows what the true status of our heart is.

So, back to my friend. What I told my friend is this, and now

I preach it to you. We have our other identities that we wear — we're American, we're Pennsylvania Dutch, we're a little bit country, or whatever they are, they are secondary to being a Christian. If we're Jewish and circumcised, then the law of tithing does represent something valuable to us. Now, my friend said, therefore, Christians shouldn't be obligated to tithe. This is true. But, I said before and I will say it again, Christianity is a dangerous religion in that we don't have these rules laid down for us very specifically. The beauty of legalistic systems is that your behavior is very clearly defined about what you should or shouldn't do. Now, because of Jesus' death on the cross, we are in a universalizing and catholic faith, liberated from the constraints of the law.

So it seems to me that the challenge of Christianity is to recognize that if Christ *really* paid for all of our sins, if God *really* sacrificed himself on the cross for us, if God *really* so loved the world that he gave his son to the world, if God *really* took on the form of a slave and humbled himself for us, that we respond to God by simply acknowledging God when the times are good, or calling on God only when the times are bad clearly isn't enough. Or coming to church out of a sense of being seen for social purposes *isn't enough*. Or parading your faith to others to show how superior you are *isn't enough*. Or justifying your wealth for the illusion that you are more blessed than others *isn't enough*. Or demonstrating the loopholes you have found yourself working through in life or in your career as demonstration that God loves you more than others *isn't enough*.

None of these things are really enough, and to believe these things, behaviors we often do and embody, is an elaborate way of worshiping ourselves. Instead, the demand of God upon us is so simple, yet so total, that we can either find joy or be crushed by the reality of Christ's love for us. So we have to ask ourselves, while we recognize that tithing no longer applies for us, whether tithing is even enough to demonstrate our genuine and authentic gratitude for everything God has done for us, and I don't mean all of the toys he has allowed us to have, but rather I am referring to the absolute sacrifice of himself on the cross for each and every one of us. Is making an appearance at church really enough? — And are we doing these things for the right reasons?

So we might be bound by some of the law if it really means making a sacrifice to God. For those of us who give sacrificially to the church and other charities, we know we could go out and probably get a few good lobster dinners with that money for ourselves. Maybe the Levitical codes that forbid us from shellfish had a point to them; that our excessiveness and the demands of the lifestyles that we want are the obstacles really sitting between where we are now and living a life that is heart-circumcised.

In Case of Rapture, We'll be on Land!

Daniel 7; 1 Thessalonians 4:13-18; Matthew 25:1-13 (Proper 27)

Death is a subject that is not comfortable to talk about. Most of you know that at weddings I like to say the prayer of Saint Francis, which concludes with the line "for it is in dying that we are born to eternal life," and I like to use Revelation 21 as my preaching text at most weddings, which is the image of a bride prepared for her husband on her wedding day as a symbol of the Kingdom of God. A few years ago, I was meeting with a couple for premarital counseling and the bride objected to the inclusion of both the Prayer of St. Francis and Revelation 21 in the wedding ceremony because they had the word "death" in them.

I said to her, but both of these are about overcoming death — and the triumph over death is part of what the Christian faith is about — as Revelation 21 reads that "death and pain will be no more, for these former things have passed away." It didn't matter. So when I asked this woman, who is about 35 years older than me, what her thoughts were about making final decisions about her new husband's life, since making end of life decisions is a right and privilege that one gets when you get married, she didn't want to talk about it. In fact, it wasn't that she didn't want to talk about it, she refused to talk about it. That day I told a woman in her 70s, as gently as possible, that I didn't think she was responsible enough to get married, and I never saw or heard from her again.

I want to be clear, I don't fault folks for being uncomfortable with the idea of death. There is probably no topic or reality of human life that has created more anxiety throughout history than death. In our Epistle reading, we find Saint Paul writing to the church in Thessalonica about death, and the early church there is struggling with the idea of death. While they were waiting for Jesus to return, they wondered, what about our faithful brothers and sisters in Christ who die while waiting? Do they get to miss out on what will be the most important event in human history?

In his writing, Saint Paul gives his famous teaching, likely making reference to the images of Daniel 7 and elsewhere in the Old Testament, where the true believers who have died are taken up to the clouds to meet with Jesus along with those who are the living believers in the event known as "The Rapture." The thing is, that in Old Testament allusions to an ascension of individuals, it is a *spiritual* ascension, and not a literal one.

Now, so much of our popular religious imagination about the end of the world, especially in the United States, is based upon a literal understanding of this teaching, a literal understanding that betrays the Jewish meanings of these words—in fact, just this past week I was behind an old station wagon nearby that read, "In Case of Rapture, Vehicle Will Become Unmanned." How the first Christians (who still identified themselves as Jews) would have heard and understood these words of scripture, was not that we would literally be taken up to the clouds, but we will be spiritually "raised" with the New Creation that is Now Occurring with the second coming of Jesus.

In other words, the Jewish ears would have heard Paul's words say that those who have died have a special and unique role to play in the coming of Jesus—whenever that may be. And so, too, with us, we may not live to see the return of Jesus, but we know that we all as individuals and as a community have a very important role to play in the process of the world preparing for Jesus to come again to begin the world again in a new way and to restore justice to the world. If we are literally raised to the clouds, it makes no difference how we prepare for the world to be re-created anew; the idea of literally meeting Jesus in the clouds appeals to many because it lets us opt out of taking the second coming seriously in that it means that we do not really have a responsibility to the world to make it a better place. If we meet Jesus in the clouds, we serve a selfish and self-centered version of Christianity, not one that really believes that Jesus was telling the truth when he said, "Behold, I am making all things new."

Instead, we are called to be spiritually raised in *this* life with the hope that we will be raised to meet Christ at his new coming. For Saint Paul, the scheme of history is that we are living in the time between the resurrection and the second coming, and, again, we all have an important role to play in taking up our own cross in the forward movement of history. And if we take the challenge of Christianity seriously, we too follow Christ in crucifixion and death, and burial, and raising. We join with Christ in ministry with him, we join with Christ in death, and we join with him in being raised.

Our hope is that in death, we will be resurrected from the grave as raised voices in a great chorus of praise. But we have hard work to do in this life, to clothe the naked, to feed the hungry, to heal the sick, to educate our children, to enlighten the ignorant, to pray without ceasing, and to preach the Gospel: to speak truth to power and to wrestle with principalities, powers, and spiritual wickedness in high places. Christ does *not* call us to retreat into the clouds while taking up our own cross. This is to say that *our work is here*, not in the sky; our deaths are not in vain so long as we accept the invitation that is our right to refuse, a challenge to make our lives a reversal of the death of this world that is perpetually passing away. The challenge is to bring life where there is death; to bring hope where there is none; to bring love where there is hate; and to be instruments of peace.

*

While all of this might give us some theological or Biblical framework for thinking about, or re-thinking death, it does not necessarily make us any less anxious about the reality of death.

Some of you know that I am someone who has struggled with depression for most of my life, and death is something that my mind often wanders towards. In some ways, I have trained myself not to think about death too much, but the lure of the infinite eternity of time that we may conceive when we occasionally peer into the idea of death is overwhelming—and it is overwhelming because it is frightening to me.

There is a legend that the infamous Confederate General, Thomas J. Jackson—"Stonewall" Jackson—said that he did not fear death because his faith taught him that he should feel as safe at battle as he does at night sleeping in his bed. When asked to explain this some more, he replied that since God has already planned the hour of his death, he is not in a position to cheat the wisdom of God in this choice of time. He can only make good with the time that he has.

As you may know, General Jackson was shot by friendly fire and a few days later developed pneumonia, and, as the story goes, in his last breaths he issued his final military orders, and paused mid-sentence, with a smile on his face, said, "Let us cross over the river, and rest under the shade of the trees." With these words, Stonewall Jackson passed away, on May 10, 1863.

The stories of our loved ones who have gone peacefully are comforting to us. The stories of those who have gone very suddenly before us, or in agony, can be disturbing to us and distract us from seeing the good of the lives lived before the end, or the "dash" that is placed between the year of birth and the year of death on someone's tombstone. Our legacy must be to live faithfully that while none of us will ever escape human death, our hope is wrapped up in our challenge that we can become part of the New Creation that is Now Occurring in Christ, preparing the universe to welcome back its King, and our Lord, as a brother in ministry and mission. We may find rest in death, and cross the river to sit under the trees, but this life is entangled with the mission planting the seeds.

*

It may be irresponsible, but I have no burial plans made. I may die tomorrow, and I'm sorry if I have left it to others to make funeral arrangements. I have kind of decided that I want to pay off my student loans before I make plans to dispose of my body when it dies!

I like to walk around our church cemetery from time to time, and the longer I am pastor at this church the more I recognize family names and know a few of the folks buried here. I like to think of church cemeteries as like a field full of seeds. When my body is planted into the ground, it is my hope that the church continues to change and that the church transfigures and blooms into something completely New, and something radically different, shedding its old skins, with the old ways dying and welcoming in the new ways. Too often, though, we see the communion of saints and cloud of witnesses around us calling us to keep the church in a kind of captivity to the past. The dead do not call us to death, but they are witnesses to us of the challenge posed by Jesus that we live life to the fullest, and by this we are called to make it possible for others to live their lives as fully as possible.

Instead, we want seeds to sprout, and to bloom, and to grow, and to pollinate, and to continue to flower and harvest beyond anything we could have done in this life. But we must prime the ground even as we sow the seeds of our bodies for the future Kingdom.

What are You Doing on June 13, 2015?[1]

Matthew 25:14-30 (Proper 28)

This story is one of the familiar parables of Jesus, though it isn't one of the most famous of Jesus' teaching. A slave owner gives one slave five talents; to another slave, two talents; and to a third slave, one talent, when he is about to go on a long journey. After some time the slave owner returns, and the slave to whom five talents was given somehow had ten total talents, and the one to whom two was given somehow now had four, and the slave owner says that these slaves are trustworthy and that he trusts them to put them in charge of things. But the slave to which was given one, buried the money and kept it safe, and only had *one* to show to the master, and the master curses the slave for not making more money with the one talent. The master uses harsh words: that the talents he has saved shall be taken and given to the more industrious servants, and the lazy slave will be thrown into the darkness, "where there will be gnashing of teeth." *This* is what the Kingdom of God is like, Jesus instructs.

This parable is so deeply entrenched in our culture that the word "talent," as in "talent show," *America's Got Talent*, or saying that someone is "talented" comes from the way in which Jesus speaks of "talents" in this parable. The word "talent" here is referring to an ancient way of measuring weight, and was a typical way of measuring the mass of precious metals—Jesus even makes reference to the talent being gold in the scripture. But this passage of scripture has been interpreted to mean "talents" in the sense of the non-monetary gifts that we all have. In other words—and I am sure you have heard this sermon before, all the way back to childhood lessons in Sunday School—that God gives us gifts and talents that we don't know about. But we have to use our talents for God and for the church, and the more we use what we're good at, the more we realize what gifts we have that we didn't have.

When I first started thinking about pursuing ordained ministry, this parable of Jesus was brought up to me constantly. I was convinced from the beginning that I was not really called to preach, because I did not like to stand in front of people and talk. I couldn't imagine that I would know enough about the Bible or have enough life experience that anyone would care what I have to say from the pulpit. In fact, after I stepped down from my first church I was pretty convinced that I should never step back into a pulpit again: I felt like no one was listening to what I was saying, and I felt like I had no point of reference for the people in that congregation. It probably didn't help that I was still figuring out how to communicate with people outside of a university, as I had just spent the last 7 years in school to be a minister, but I left that church committed to never preaching ever again.

But things changed for me. I preached occasionally when I was invited, and then I began to be invited to preach more and more. And then, all of a sudden, I became interested in preaching again, and took a couple of advanced preaching classes, and suddenly felt called back into the pulpit. In fact, I had no interest in being ordained at one point, and suddenly the lure of the pulpit brought me back into the ministry.

I share this story not so much to trumpet my own gifts, because I know some folks think I'm a terrible preacher. But my point is that the way we have interpreted this passage of scripture is very much about our talents and our hidden talents. This idea—that we have hidden talents—is in fact a *very* Christian idea. Sometimes our life situations lead us to discover talents we never would have thought we had. I know a lot of folks who became interested in singing at a later age who had no interest in their younger years and joined a church choir only to discover that they could sing and that they really enjoyed singing. Many of us never thought of ourselves as good parents or good grandparents until we were thrown into the fire of parenting, just hoping that we didn't get burned. In fact, I think it's probably safe to say that many of the younger parents I know who are convinced they're really good parents are the ones who are probably really bad parents; I have found that convincing yourself that you're good at something before you really are is not only an easy way of being disappointed down the road but it's a way we avoid doing the hard work of earning or doing the heavy lifting of being really good at something.

I used to work with someone who had stuff about how great a mom she was all over her office and was so self-righteous about being a good mother, and even had a license plate that said "Supermom" on it. You know the type: the parents who think their kids can do no wrong; one time I had to ask myself if we were talking about the same child with her when she was telling me how great her son is, how he had a nearly 4.0 in high school (even though I knew she harassed the teachers if they dared give her darling son an A minus in anything), and how pretty his girlfriends are, just as I was getting ready to go visit the kid in jail for drug possession. You all know the kind of parent I'm talking about! My point is that often the things we think we're really good at are not what we are really good at, but if we're honest and we work hard we discover that there are other things we're good at.

And this seems to be the message of the story, in the way it's usually read: That if you are given a talent or two, you can discover that you have four. Or if you're really talented, and are given five talents, you have to come up with even more talents: when the Master returns, you should be ready to show ten. But if you have just one talent, and hide it somewhere, and the Master discovers upon his return that you still only have one, you are lazy and incompetent, and, so the story implies, you deserve to go to Hell.

What I don't buy about this interpretation is that we all know that it's easier to make money if you have money. Now, it's also easy to spend the money, too, if you have money. But if you're investing, and you begin with $500, you are probably able to take on more risk in your investments than if you only have $100. In fact, if you only have $100 to your name, you might not try to invest the money at all, because you wouldn't want to lose it all if the market crashes.

Some things to keep in mind about this story are that we're talking about a master and his slaves, not an employer and free employees, and not a father with his sons. The story is kind of ridiculous on this level, because only a fool would let his slaves hold onto his money. A talent, we should keep in mind, was a significant amount of money. So one talent might have been about 150 times what a typical wage-earner would have received for his work for an entire year. The slave who received one talent was receiving 150 times what he would have earned if he were a free man; the one who received five talents would have received 750 times the yearly pay of a free worker.

Now, let me turn this story around a little bit. Jesus' story in the scriptures says that the rich man is about to leave for a journey when he entrusts these riches to his three slaves. And Jesus says that when the rich slave-owner returns, his return comes "after a long time," and when he came home, "the master of those slaves came and settled accounts with them." When I first hear the story, I think that the journey is maybe a couple weeks, a couple months even. But Jesus says that it is a long time. How long, we don't know, it's just a story. But it is a "long time."

Picture this. Suppose that the slaves thought that the Master was gone so long that the slaves assumed that he really wasn't going to come back, and the slaves started investing the money as if they were free men. The slave with five talents eventually had a value of ten talents; and the one with two eventually increased his net worth to four talents. Not too shabby, even if the Master was away for ten years or longer.

When the Master returns, these slaves can't believe it! Their Master has returned not just to check his bank account numbers, but to "settle accounts with them." Because the Master owns the slaves, everything that is theirs is his. Imagine what must have been going through these rich slaves' minds: all of the sacrifices and hard work they made to make this money grow, all of their riches, all this enormous wealth! And not just some wealth, but such unimaginable wealth that for the one slave, it was more than he would have earned in over 700 years as a free man! Now he has to turn it all back to the slave-owner, who was gone so long they didn't think he was going to return.

The Master is jubilant, because, even though the slaves took risks with the money, the Master returns richer than he was before. So I imagine the slaves, saying, in shock, not so much proud, but humble, "Master, you handed over to me five talents; see, I have made five more talents." And the Master jovially says, "Well done, good and trustworthy slave; you have been trustworthy in a *few* things, I will put you in charge of many things; enter into the joy of your master!" Instead of sharing in the wealth, the slave-owner says, since you have doubled my money, you've done alright, so now I won't whip you when I get angry. You're still less than human to me, but I'll be nice to you now. This exchange is not so much one of congratulations but one of hopes unfulfilled and harsh sarcasm.

In other words, the slaves thought they had earned all of this money for themselves, and they are suddenly reminded that they are in fact slaves, and not only is their money not their own, because it never really was in the first place, but they don't get to reap the benefits.

But one slave believed that the Master would return and he saved the money, hiding it to keep it safe. Not taking risks or liberties with his slave-owner's money, he actually believed that the master would return, but now seeing that he has returned and taken the money back from the others, the slave says to the master: "I know you did not earn this money honestly, and I know you did not invest in honestly, but when you gave it to me, out of fear and respect for you as my slave-master, I did not risk it. I kept it honestly, I did not spend it, but I sustained it. You gave less to me because you did not trust me with more, and out of respect for you I did what you expected. Here's your talent of gold, my Lord!"

The Master is mad, and gives the famous line of the parable: *For all those who have, more will be given, and they will have an abundance; but from those who have nothing, even what they have will be taken away.* The Master casts the lazy slave out into the "outer darkness, where there will be weeping and gnashing of teeth." What strikes me is that the slaves who earned the riches still had nothing as well, and even having nothing, what they did have was taken away from them.

To Jesus' claim that this story is "what the Kingdom of God is like," could it be that Jesus is not really siding with the industrious slaves, but instead the Kingdom of God sides with the conservative servant who, even in loyalty to his master, angers him for doing pretty much what he expected him to do?

We've all been in situations where you may have had two or three choices, and no matter what choice you make your boss is going to be angry. Or the boss might be happy with what you have done and took credit? Or even that you're doing the right thing and someone takes what you're doing to be the opposite? It stinks to be in that situation, and perhaps what Jesus' parable is saying is *not* the typical reading, which takes the side of the slave-owner who exploits his slaves, but instead the parable has God siding with the poor servant who did what he was supposed to do, who treated other people's talents with respect and kept them safe.

And most importantly, placing this parable in context with the rest of the chapter of Matthew 25, the so-called lazy servant is the *only* one who really believed that the Master would return.

The other slaves didn't believe he would return, and encountered a harsh reminder when he did. The parable right before this one—to consider the story in the context of the Gospel of Matthew—ends with the line, "Keep watch, because you do not know the day or the hour" (Matt. 25: 13), and the very next line after our passage of scripture begins, "When the Son of Man comes in glory ... he will separate people from one another as a shepherd separates sheep from the goats" (25: 31-32). My point is that the so-called lazy servant wasn't too surprised that the master returned, and he spoke the truth to the master, whereas the others were too embarrassed and ashamed that they just continued on in the shock of their own status as slaves.

We are to be on guard and ready for Jesus to come again. So very often, we start planning stuff for the future, often so distant that we would be disappointed if Jesus came to interrupt our plans. Not too long ago I had someone call and ask me to schedule a wedding for June 13, 2015. I said to the woman on the phone, "did you just say 2015?" "Well," she said, "we need to save up some money and I want to get married on the second Saturday in June, and the place I want to get married is booked for that Saturday in 2014." I told her that it's my experience that when couples schedule weddings that far in advance it's usually a defense tactic for the guy to buy some time to figure a way out of the wedding.

Thinking about things into the future, we can all consider forthcoming events that we look forward to: We look forward to seeing our grandchildren and children graduate from school, or get married, or have children themselves. Or we look forward to our retirements. Or we look forward to the vacation we've been saving up for. The question we have to face, then, is whether these plans, which are all legitimate things to look forward to, are really an elaborate way of declaring that we have no faith that Jesus will come again? What if Jesus returns in the first week of December? Would one of our first thoughts be that we still need to get some Christmas shopping done? Are we really waiting in expectation, or is the future only something whose hopes are built in what we can *earn*, or what our children can *earn* or *do*, and not in a faith of the return of Christ? Are we really ready to cancel our season passes to the local amusement park for next year? And are we really willing to close the church and enter into a truly new Kingdom when Jesus returns? Or will we just keep preaching the old Gospel stories, because we think we know them?

When I actually checked my calendar for June 13, 2015, and I did check my calendar, what I found was that the second Saturday in June is always the date of the Penn Central Conference (United Church of Christ) annual meeting. The very fact that I can think about this date in the future, and that I have the annual meeting programmed in my electronic datebook to recur, demonstrates that our routines of going about our lives and our business forbids any reality of the actual return of Jesus. I'm actually already committed to attend the Conference meeting that Saturday, and just by virtue of the fact that I can think this way assumes a kind of religious dishonesty, that as I expect to be present at the annual conference that weekend, I also expect that Jesus won't return by then, as well.

Our lesson from Jesus today demonstrates that the one who believes in the return is the one who has the least to lose and has placed the least amount of self-importance into his possessions and in his money. And the one who is believed to be lazy, and the one who is believed to be selfish, and the one who is cast out into hell by the mainstream of society is really the one who is faithfully waiting.

Afterword

Thomas J. J. Altizer

Nothing is more challenging to us than is preaching itself, nor anything more difficult to write than a book on preaching, or even a collection of sermons intended to embody genuine preaching. At no point did Barth and Tillich so decisively establish themselves as theologians than they did in their published sermons, and virtually anyone could respond to these sermons, or anyone who could actually hear. Pastor Rodkey's *Too Good to Be True* is and is not a book of sermons, if only because it is difficult to imagine hearing this book, unless perhaps one intends to hear it as a liturgical celebration, and above all a celebration of that Easter which embodies the New Life. But Pastor Rodkey can speak against his own preaching, as he does in his assault on German Christianity, a Christianity centered in the Crucifixion, and one that gave us that death of God theology which he so admires.

The truth is that Easter and Resurrection are hollow and unreal apart from the Crucifixion, a hollowness fully manifest in that popular Christianity which Pastor Rodkey so fully assaults; so, too, a New Life is wholly unreal apart from a New Death, for that is the death that is wholly absent in all common or popular Christianity. Despite this Christianity, resurrection is a rather minor motif both in the New Testament and in the more powerful expressions of Christianity, or is so when it is dissociated from crucifixion, as it never is in either Paul or the Gospels. In popular Christianity resurrection simply passed into immortality, hence becoming wholly pagan and non-Biblical, and also profoundly unchallenging, as we can see most concretely in popular Christian art. And if we are to take preaching with genuine seriousness, then we must never depart from that Kierkegaard who is our supreme preacher, a Kierkegaard for whom genuine preaching is always a profound offense, and one that cannot be heard apart from such offense.

As a rebel against all established Christianity, I also rebel against what little I know as seminary teaching, which appears and particularly so in its effects to teach the very opposite of genuine Christianity, which one can observe in simply leafing through the popular books on Christianity in our bookstores. Here, the Devil openly rules, and it is not insignificant that the Devil or Satan is so absent from popular Christianity, just as is damnation itself. Many if not most Christians associate Satan and damnation with the Old Testament, where they are wholly absent, and it is Jesus who speaks of Satan more than any other Biblical or ancient figure. This is a Jesus who is silent in popular Christianity, so, too, is silent the apocalyptic Jesus, which most critical modern New Testament scholarship has demonstrated is the Jesus of Paul and the synoptic Gospels. Popular Christianity is both removed from and indifferent to Biblical scholarship, and the largest of all Protestant bodies, the Southern Baptist Conference, could assault Biblical scholarship, and did so with such power as to induce a schism in the Southern Baptist Church.

This is the situation in which Radical Christianity is virtually unknown in our country if not in the world itself, but we can know Kierkegaard, and Barth, and Tillich as Radical Christians, and if we accept critical New Testament scholarship, we can know Jesus as a Radical Christian, and Paul, too. So, too, genuine Christian preaching must be a preaching of Radical Christianity, one to which Pastor Rodkey is clearly committed, but I suspect that such preaching is rare indeed, and would meet with little support in most of our churches. Can this be true? Or have few of our Christians ever encountered radical preaching, or encountered Radical Christianity itself, or even a preaching in genuine continuity with the Bible? While we can encounter a seemingly great commitment to the Bible, is that commitment real, or real as a commitment to anything that is actually the Bible, or actually heard as the Bible to a genuine listener?

One of the great illusions of our world is that common or popular Christianity is Biblical Christianity, and that an absolute commitment to the literal interpretation of the Bible is an absolute commitment to the Bible itself, a literal interpretation that didn't even come into existence until the advent of the modern secular world, and that was itself a violent reaction against modern Biblical scholarship. One can amuse oneself by visiting Christian bookstores and discovering that most of them contain no critical or scholarly books on the Bible, or serious books of any kind on either religion or the Bible. Here, we can easily encounter that pabulum which Pastor Rodkey so forcefully attacks, but then we can recognize that most of us today have no point of contact with anything genuinely Biblical or genuinely religious, and this is true of our world as it was not of previous worlds. Just read a sermon of Jonathan Edwards, and do so with the awareness that he was an enormously popular preacher, perhaps the most admired and popular preacher of his day. Who could imagine a Jonathan Edwards in one of our pulpits today? Or imagine him as a popular theologian today? Is he even taught in our seminaries? And has our theological world ever been at a lower point than it is today? Could it have been this bad even in the Dark Ages? And how many are concerned about that today? Can we really believe that ours is a Christian world and that the great majority of Americans are Christian?

References

Pentecosting: Preaching the Death of God
This essay benefitted from feedback at the Subverting the Norm II conference held at Drury University, Springfield, MO, in April, 2013.

1. David Buttrick, *Homiletic: Moves and Structures* (Philadelphia: Fortress, 1987), 193.

2. Charles Winquist, *Practical Hermeneutics* (Atlanta: Scholars', 1980), 88.

3. Gabriel Vahanian, *Wait Without Idols* (New York: Braziller, 1964), 231.

4. I explain and explore this in more detail in my essay, "Methodist Heretic: Thomas Altizer at Emory University," in *Methodist History* 49.1 (2010): 37-50.

5. On "necrophilia," see Mary Daly and Jane Caputi, *Websters' First New Intergalactic Wickedary of the English Language* (Boston: Beacon, 1987), 83-84.

6. Ephesians 6:12.

7. Friedrich Nietzsche, *The Gay Science*, trans. W. Kaufmann (New York: Vintage, 1974), 125.

8. See Mark C. Taylor and Dietrich Lammerts, *Grave Matters* (London: Reakion, 2002).

9. Christopher Rodkey, *The Synaptic Gospel* (Lanham, MD: University Press of America, 2012), 68-70, 73ff.

10. Cf. Daly and Caputi, *Wickedary* (1987), 96.

11. 1 Corinthians 1:23.

12. Mark 15:34.

13. For a fuller critique on this point, please see Jeffrey Robins and Christopher Rodkey, "Beating 'God' to Death: Radical Theology and the New Atheism," *Religion and the New Atheism: A Critical Appraisal*, ed. Amarnath Amarasingam (Leiden: Brill, 2010), 25-36.

14. This news was reported widely, for example, in *The*

Washington Post, see http://articles.washingtonpost.com/2012-07-17/national/35489147_1_florida-pastor-terry-jones-quran-resolution (accessed online, 28. December 2012).

15. I wish to recognize before my critics do, the obvious: Not all atheists behave in this way, and European atheism functions quite differently than American atheism, as Žižek writes succinctly in his March 12, 2006, *New York Times* editorial, "Defenders of the Faith" (http://www.nytimes.com/2006/03/12/opinion/12zizek.html?_r=0).

16. Genesis 4:15.

17. Peter Rollins, *Insurrection* (New York: Howard, 2011), 21.

18. Paul Tillich, *The Courage to Be* (New Haven: Yale UP, 1980), 190

19. Matthew 28:2, 27:51.

20. Peter Rollins, *Insurrection*, 180.

21. Vahanian, *Wait Without Idols*, 236.

22. Davidson Loehr, *America, Fascism, and God: Sermons from a Heretical Preacher* (White River Junction, VT: Chelsea Green, 2005), xviii.

23. Tillich, *The Courage to Be*; Mary Daly, *Amazon Grace: Re-Calling the Courage to Sin Big* (New York: Palgrave, 2006).

24. Nietzsche, *The Gay Science*, 124.

25. John 20:22.

26. Vahanian, *Wait Without Idols*, 233.

27. Dow Kirkpatrick, "A Sermon on the Death of God," *Christian Advocate* 11.4 (24. Feb. 1966), 11-12.

28. Gayle Worland, "Rev. Dow Napier Kirkpatrick, 87: Church Leader, Social Activist" [obituary], *Chicago Tribune* (14. March 2004), online. Accessed 5. January 2012.

29. Paul Tillich, *The Irrelevance and Relevance of the Christian Message* (Cleveland: Pilgrim, 1996); Thomas Altizer, *The Call to Radical Theology*, ed. Lissa McCullough (Albany, NY: SUNY UP, 2013), 4-5.

30. John 2:1-11.

31. Vahanian, *Wait Without Idols*, 243.

32. On the apocalyptic ethics of the beatitudes, see Altizer, *The Call to Radical Theology*, 51-65.

33. Thomas Altizer, *The Apocalyptic Trinity* (New York: Palgrave, 2012), 50.

34. Paul Van Buren, *The Edge of Language* (London: SCM, 1972) and Gabriel Vahanian, *Anonymous God*, trans. Nöelle Vahanian (Aurora, CO: Davies, 2002), 112.

35. Buttrick, *Homiletic*, 117.

36. See, for example, Jeremiah Wright's sermons in *What Makes You So Strong?*, ed. Jini Kilgore (Valley Forge: Judson, 1993.)

37. Jeffrey Robbins, *In Search of a Non-Dogmatic Theology* (Aurora, CO: Davies, 2003), 38-39.

38. Edith Guffey, quoted in Thomas Dipko, ed., *Affirming Faith: A Confirmand's Journal*, 2nd rev. and updated ed. (Cleveland: United Church Press, 2008), 13.

39. Adam Kotsko, *Awkwardness* (Winchester, UK: O-Books, 2010), 86.

40. Phil Snider discusses this reversal in more detail, invoking the work of Peter Gomes, John Caputo, and Carl Raschke in Snider, *Preaching after God* (Eugene, OR: Wipf & Stock, 2012), 36, 44, 62.

41. Joseph Fort Newton, *Sermons and Lectures: Delivered at the Liberal Christian Church, Grand Rapids, Iowa* (Cedar Rapids, 1919), "Nietzsche: Apostle of Anti-Christ," III.

42. Congregational Vitality and Discipleship Ministry Team of the Local Church Ministries of the United Church of Christ, "SAMUEL: Preaching in the United Church of Christ," online, accessible at http://www.ucc.org/worship/samuel; Richard Swanson, *Provoking the Gospel of Matthew* (Cleveland: Pilgrim, 2007), *Provoking the Gospel of Mark* (Cleveland: Pilgrim, 2005); *Provoking the Gospel of Luke* (Cleveland: Pilgrim, 2006), and *Provoking the Gospel of John* (Cleveland: Pilgrim, 2010); Paul Nuechterlein, ed. and

comp., "Girardian Reflections on the Lectionary," accessible online at http://girardianlectionary.net.

43. The blogging community, *An und für sich*, maintained by Adam Kotsko, may be found online at http://itself .wordpress.com.

The Jokulhaups

1. An explanation of Magic: The Gathering may be found at the publisher's website, "What is Magic: The Gathering?": http://www.wizards.com/Magic/tcg/NewtoMagic.aspx?x=mt g/tcg/newtomagic/whatismagic.

2. An image of this particular playing card may be found at the publisher's website: http://gatherer.wizards.com/pages/card /Details.aspx?multiverseid=14653.

3. The Revised Common Lectionary texts for The Reign of Christ, the final Sunday of the season after Pentecost, are Jeremiah 23:1-6, Psalm 46, Colossians 1:1-20, Luke 23:33-43 (with an additional alternate reading of Luke 1:68-79).

He Touched Me at the Airport

1. For an article on the cultural significance of "Doctorin' the Tardis" by The Timelords (also known as the KLF), see http://en.wikipedia.org/wiki/Doctorin%27_the_Tardis.

2. Genesis 3:14.

3. Heraclitus, Fragment 41.

Queer Accusation!

1. This phrase refers to Chris Farley's *Saturday Night Live* meme.

'Christmas' isn't in the Bible?

1. See "When Americans Banned Christmas," The Week, online, accessed 15. April 2013. http://theweek.com /article/index/222676/when-americans-banned-christmas.

References

Lord, You have Come to the Lakeshore

1. This title refers to the fantastic hymn, "Tú has venido a la orilla" by Cesáreo Gabaráin.
2. SAMUEL Sermon Seeds, United Church of Christ, 2001.

The Be-Attitudes

1. The video is online, posted by a very biased source, at http://www.youtube.com/watch?v=6wpCCSZ22fQ.
2. See Paul Tillich's *The Courage to Be*.
3. Galatians 3:28.
4. Cf. Mary Daly, *Outercourse* (New York: Harper San Francisco, 1992), 31.

You are the Salt of the Road!

1. Cf. Bernard Jones, *Freemason's Guide and Compendium*, new and rev. ed. (Exeter, England: Barnes & Noble, 1986) 19ff.
2. Acts 2:17.

Between Necrophilia and Biophilia!

1. 1 Corinthians 1:23.
2. Cite Mary Daly, *Pure Lust* (New York: Harper San Francisco, 1984), 74-75.
3. *Ibid.* 106ff.
4. *The Passion of the Christ*, dir. Mel Gibson (2004).

The Good Catastrophe

1. Here I am referencing the events surrounding the Economic Stimulus Act of 2008; this sermon was preached before the economic crash that happened later in 2008.
2. Bob Dylan, "Gotta Serve Somebody," *Slow Train Coming* (Columbia Records, 1979).
3. Christopher Rodkey, *The Synaptic Gospel* (Lanham, MD: University Press of America, 2012), 69-70, 73ff.
4. Bobby McFerrin, "Don't Worry, Be Happy," *Cocktail (Original*

Motion Picture Soundtrack) (Elektra, 1988).
5.   Karen Lafferty, "Seek Ye First."
6.   J. R. R. Tolkien, "On Fairy-Stories," *Essays Presented to Charles Williams*, ed. C. S. Lewis (Grand Rapids, MI: Eerdmans, 1968), 60ff; Christopher Rodkey, *In the Horizon of the Infinite* (Ph.D. diss., Drew University, 2008), 313-320.

Preparing Again for the Death of God
1.   *Time* magazine, cover, April 8, 1966.
2.   Bob Dylan, "The Times They are a-Changin'," *The Times They Are a-Changin'* (Columbia, 1964).
3.   See Robbins and Rodkey, "Beating God to Death."

Re-membering the Dis-membered
1.   Anonymous, "He is Lord."
2.   Cf. Genesis, god setting up with snake.
3.   Job 1:6ff.

Nicodemus' Secret
1.   This is a common belief in esoteric Christianity; see, for example, Edouard Schuré, *Jesus, the Last Great Initiate*, trans. T. Rothwell (Chicago: Yogi, 1908).
2.   Matthew 8:21-22.
3.   John 7:52-53.
4.   John 19:39ff.

Silent but Violent!
1.   R. Swanson, *Provoking the Gospel of Matthew*, p. 116.
2.   Cf. Nietzsche, *The Gay Science*, 125.

Too Good to be True!
1.   Jane Chapman and Karma Wilson, *Bear Wants More* (New York: McElderry, 2003).

Where's the Death Certificate?

1. This fringe movement continues as the "Birthers"; their website is http://birthers.org.
2. The details of this game may be found on Yahoo! sports online (http://sports.yahoo.com/mlb/boxscore?gid=31050112 2) and a video of these events is also on YouTube (http://www.youtube.com/watch?feature=player_embedded &v=NW8ko4x5ukg).

This Place Stinks!

1. Mother Teresa, *Come Be My Light* (New York: Doubleday, 2007), 1.

Good News to the World the Church has Hurt

1. Here I am discussing Sister Barbara Sheehan, SP, director of the Urban Clinical Pastoral Education Consortium in Chicago.

The World has Already Ended!

1. Harold Camping later admitted he was wrong, as reported by the Huffington Post (http://www.huffingtonpost. com/2012/03/09/harold-camping-admits-hes-wrong_n _1335232.html)
2. *New York Daily News*, May 19, 2011.
3. See, for example, the Wikipedia article on this subject at http://en.wikipedia.org/wiki/Great_Disappointment.
4. Bruce Epperly, "Going Up?", Patheos, accessed online at http://www.patheos.com/Resources/Additional-Resources/Going-Up-Reflections-on-Ascension-Day-Bruce-Epperly-05-30-2011.

You Put Your Weeds in There!

1. The title is punning on the *Saturday Night Live* gag of the same name that has been repeated in other Adam Sandler

films.

2. Rob Bell, *Love Wins* (New York: HarperOne, 2012).

3. As reported in *New York Daily News*: http://www.nydailynews.com/news/national/chad-holtz-methodist-church-pastor-north-carolina-fired-questioning-hell-exists-article-1.118345. Since then, however, the pastor in question, Chad Holtz, has changed his mind, as reported by the Huffington Post online (http://www.huffingtonpost.com/john-shore/chad-holtz-pastor-fired-for-doubting_b_1683722.html).

Slapped by Your Grandma!

1. In Genesis 1.

2. René Girard, *Things Hidden Since the Foundation of the World* (Continuum, 2003).

3. The video of this happening may be found at http://www.youtube.com/watch?v=IQjLcda2CTQ.

Do You Want Steak or Salad?

1. Girard, *Things Hidden Since the Foundation of the World*, 144-146.

Worshiping the Golden Calf

1. Vahanian, *Anonymous God*, 112.

2. Cf. *Ibid.*

3. William Hamilton, *On Taking God out of the Dictionary* (New York: McGraw-Hill, 1974).

What are You Doing on June 13, 2015?

1. For context, this sermon was delivered on November 13, 2011.

About the author and contributors

Peter Rollins, the author of the foreword, is one of the most controversial and most-sought contemporary Christian speakers, known for his gifts in storytelling and his "transformance art." Peter is a graduate (B.A.[hons.], M.A., and Ph.D.) from Queen's University, Belfast, and is currently a research associate with the Irish School of Ecumenics in Trinity College, Dublin. Dr. Rollins's books include *How (Not) to Speak of God* (2006), *The Fidelity of Betrayal* (2008), *The Orthodox Heretic* (2009), *Insurrection* (2011), and *The Idolatry of God* (2013). His website is found online at http://peterrollins.net.

Thomas J. J. Altizer, who contributed the afterword, is one of the century's most important and infamous theologians. A graduate of the University of Chicago (B.A., M.A., and Ph.D.), Dr. Altizer became one of the United States' most controversial intellectuals while teaching at Emory University, and spent the majority of his career teaching at Stony Brook University; there he holds the title Professor Emeritus of Religious Studies. The author of numerous books, they include *Oriental Mysticism and Biblical Eschatology* (1961), *Mircea Eliade and the Dialectic of the Sacred* (1963), *The Gospel of Christian Atheism* (1966), *The New Apocalypse* (1967), *The Descent into Hell* (1970), *The Self-Embodiment of God* (1977), *Total Presence* (1980), *History as Apocalypse* (1985), *The Genesis of God* (1993), *The Contemporary Jesus* (1997), *The New Gospel of Christian Atheism* (2001), *Godhead and the Nothing* (2003), *Living the Death of God* (2006), *The Apocalyptic Trinity* (2012), and *The Call to Radical Theology* (2013). He is also an occasional blogger for *An und für sich* (http://itself.wordpress.com).

Christopher D. Rodkey is Pastor of St. Paul's United Church of Christ in Dallastown, Pennsylvania, where he lives with his spouse and three children. He teaches at Penn State York and Lancaster Theological Seminary. He is a graduate of Saint Vincent College (B.A.), the University of Chicago (M.Div.), Meadville Lombard Theological School (D.Min.), and Drew University (Ph.D.). He is widely published in numerous journals and edited collections, and is author of *The Synaptic Gospel: Teaching the Brain to Worship* (2012) and blogs at *An und für sich* (http://itself. wordpress.com).

CHRISTIAN
ALTERNATIVE

Throughout the two thousand years of Christian tradition there have been, and still are, groups and individuals that exist in the margins and upon the edge of faith. But in Christianity's contrapuntal history it has often been these outcasts and pioneers that have forged contemporary orthodoxy out of former radicalism as belief evolves to engage with and encompass the ever-changing social and scientific realities. Real faith lies not in the comfortable certainties of the Orthodox, but somewhere in a half-glimpsed hinterland on the dirt track to Emmaus, where the Death of God meets the Resurrection, where the supernatural Christ meets the historical Jesus, and where the revolution liberates both the oppressed and the oppressors.

Welcome to Christian Alternative... a space at the edge where the light shines through.